- 2

STALKING SHADOWS

About the Author

Debi Chestnut has been able to see and speak to ghosts her whole life. A paranormal researcher for more than twenty-five years, she gives lectures and conducts workshops to help people better understand paranormal activity. She resides in Michigan.

Debi Chestnut

The Most
Chilling Experiences
of a Paranormal Investigator

STALKING
SHADOWS

Llewellyn Publications
Woodbury, Minnesota

FIRST EDITION
First Printing, 2014

Cover art: Shutterstock/66377758/© Unholy Vault Designs
Cover design by Lisa Novak
Editing by Gabrielle Rose Simons

Llewellyn Publications is a registered trademark of Llewellyn Worldwide Ltd.

Library of Congress Cataloging-in-Publication Data
Chestnut, Debi.
  Stalking shadows: The most chilling experiences of a paranormal investigator / by Debi Chestnut. — First edition.
       pages   cm
  ISBN 978-0-7387-3943-4
1. Parapsychology. 2. Ghosts. 3. Haunted places. I. Title.
  BF1031.C495 2014
  133.1—dc23
                                    2014028272

Llewellyn Publications
A Division of Llewellyn Worldwide Ltd.
2143 Wooddale Drive
Woodbury, MN 55125-2989
www.llewellyn.com

Printed in the United States of America

Other books by Debi Chestnut

Is Your House Haunted?

How to Clear Your Home of Ghosts & Spirits

To Amy Glaser, my Acquisitions Editor,
and all the wonderful people at Llewellyn
who work so hard to make my job easier.

Contents

Prologue . . . xi

Chapter 1: The Man in the Mirror . . . 1

Chapter 2: Nathanial . . . 15

Chapter 3: The Ancestral Home . . . 29

Chapter 4: The Screaming Lady . . . 37

Chapter 5: Franklin's Story . . . 45

Chapter 6: The Weeping Woman . . . 61

Chapter 7: What's Going On Around Here? . . . 69

Chapter 8: The House of Horrors . . . 91

Chapter 9: The Haunted Land . . . 103

Chapter 10: The Cemetery of Restless Souls . . . 117

Chapter 11: The Haunted Church . . . 143

Chapter 12: Home Sweet Haunted Home . . . 155

Chapter 13: When Darkness Comes to Play . . . 175

Conclusion . . . 195

PROLOGUE

If the world of the paranormal were a basement, what an incredible place it would be to explore.

You'd creep down the stairs and switch on the light, which is probably just a naked 75-watt bulb dangling from a thin, dusty, electrical wire in the ceiling, and survey your surroundings.

Over by a high, narrow window in which soft rays of sunlight slither through fraying curtains, you might see a group of light beings such as angels, spirit guides, and guardians, sorting through the boxes of memorabilia that make up people's lives in search of those who need help or guidance.

Next to an old dresser and steamer trunk may sit a bookshelf lined with books; each book holds the story of someone's life, loves, disappointments and regrets, and triumphs. The last chapter reveals the details of their death, and may explain why some of them choose to interact with the world of the living—a world they once belonged to.

In the corner next to the old, worn wooden stairs that lead from the basement, you may be fortunate enough to see the spirits of departed loved ones partaking in the activities they so enjoyed when they were alive.

As you gaze at them, just beyond the memories and mementos of their lives that are stacked neatly around them, you can't help but notice that they look healthy and vibrant. They may pause to greet you or give you a friendly nod. Though your heart aches to join them, you know you can't —it's not yet your time—there are more chapters left to be written in your book of life.

As in any basement, there are the dark corners where no amount of light can reach. You know those corners are there and they make you fidget uncomfortably as your eyes fight not to peer into the darkness to see what treasures may be hiding just out of sight. You can choose to ignore them, or attempt to trick your mind into forgetting that the spirits are there, but what lies beyond the darkness does exist, and you can only fool yourself for so long.

One dark, musty corner could contain the grimy, thick crust of human suffering, agony, corruption, and man's inhumanity to man. Another gloomy corner may hold the decaying remains of natural tragedies, and the souls who were victims of such disasters.

However, for some inexplicable reason, you are drawn to the darkest, most mysterious corner of the paranormal basement. There, shrouded behind a dense veil of cobwebs and shadows, are the most contemptible and foul entities that exist—negative ghosts or spirits, demons, elementals, and other vile phantoms that aren't spoken of in the bright light of day, in the darkness of the night, or in polite company.

You fight to tear your eyes away from the gruesome creatures residing in that corner, because there is a plethora of other interesting treasures in the basement waiting patiently for you to examine them and uncover their secrets.

The paranormal basement isn't for everyone—and not a pleasant place for many. Some people even refuse to open the door to the paranormal, let alone venture down the basement stairs and explore the interesting, mysterious, and oftentimes frightening world that exists all around them, just out of sight.

But not you. If you've made it this far, you're one of the brave ones. As you take your time and explore, perhaps you radiate a divine light to help illuminate what lies within the darkest nooks and crannies of the paranormal basement, and protect you from what is to come.

You've made the choice to brush aside the veil of cobwebs and venture beyond the safety of what you know and into the deepest caverns of the paranormal.

As you make your way over to the bookshelf in the basement to peruse the titles, you can't help but wonder what lies ahead on your journey into the paranormal. I can assure you that when you descend the stairs to the paranormal basement and begin to uncover the lives of the dead, the dead know … and they hunt you down.

You walk over to the high, narrow window and curl up in an old, overstuffed chair that is covered with an afghan someone's long forgotten relative made. You choose that place because it's closest to the light—closest to what you perceive to be safety.

But don't worry, for you are not alone. I'm there with you in the paranormal basement, and the books on the shelf are mine. No, I didn't collect people's lives or souls; they came to me. They wanted their stories to be told; they want you to know what really happened, and they've chosen to tell their stories through me because I'm a psychic medium and have been able to see and communicate with ghosts for as long as I can remember.

I've been a ghost hunter for the last thirty years. I work with a team, Black River Paranormal, started by a friend of mine, Randy, and his brother.

There aren't a lot of members in our team, but the members we do have are all wonderful and dedicated investigators who share the same goal—to learn more about ghosts and spirits and other entities that exist.

Black River Paranormal also works closely with other ghost hunting teams in the area, especially A & J Ghost Hunters out of Sanilac, Michigan. We, like many other paranormal teams around the world, believe in paranormal unity. This means that we embrace working with other ghost hunting teams and sharing what we've learned on our journey. We also like learning about the experiences and theories of other paranormal investigators, which helps broaden our horizons and further understand the world of the paranormal.

So let's begin our tour of the paranormal basement.

Chapter 1

The Man in the Mirror

Every once in a while a ghost comes along that presents unique challenges. It starts out seemingly simple, and turns into something very complicated and intriguing. These challenges could range from a particularly stubborn ghost not wanting to communicate, not wanting to leave, to even speaking a foreign language and refusing to communicate in a language I can understand, or worse yet, not communicating at all.

The problem generally doesn't present itself right away, but develops over the course of my or the team's investigation. Sometimes a ghost will hide because it is afraid we're going to make it leave or harm it in some way. In other cases a ghost or spirit might try to reverse the entire situation and instead of us hunting the ghost, the ghost decides to hunt us. In still other cases, a ghost or some other type of entity may have gotten itself in a predicament and desperately needs help. In other words, a paranormal investigation can start out seemingly simple, but all of a sudden turn into something very complicated and interesting.

Such was the case when I was contacted by Randy, the head of our team, Black River Paranormal. He'd been contacted by a young man named Sam, who'd had a rather active spirit residing in his bedroom since he'd moved in six months earlier.

Pictures and posters were being ripped violently off the walls, and various items were being thrown off shelves and hurled across the bedroom. The case sounded rather basic—all signs pointed to a poltergeist.

Sam and his roommate, who wasn't experiencing any paranormal activity, lived in a second floor apartment of what used to be an antique store. Randy arranged for us to go out there on a Sunday morning.

The day of the ghost hunt dawned dark and rainy. Thunder rolled through the clouds and lightning streaked across the sky like a spiderweb as I backed out of my driveway—perfect conditions for a ghost hunt. Sam lived about an hour away, and I had to stop at a Catholic church to refill the container I used for holy water, which was another experience in itself, and should have been a clue about how the rest of the day was going to go.

When I got to the church the rain was coming down in buckets and I realized that Sunday service was going to start in a few minutes. I dashed into the church only to find about a hundred people milling around the expansive lobby and a kindly looking woman handing out some type of literature.

Keep in mind that I was dressed in a pair of blue jeans and a T-shirt with Black River Paranormal emblazoned in large letters across the front of the shirt.

Next to the woman stood a humongous waterfall and fountain.

"Can I help you, dear?" asked the woman, dressed in her Sunday finest.

"Yes, is that holy water?" I pointed to the fountain and waterfall.

"Yes it is."

"May I have some?" I asked.

She waved her hand toward the fountain. "Help yourself, honey."

"Yes, ma'am. Thank you," I said sheepishly as I filled up my container with the cool liquid.

As I was walking out the woman stopped me and read the front of my shirt. "Is everything okay, dear? Did you need us to help you?"

"Yes, ma'am. Everything is fine so far, but I'll let you know if I need any help. Thank you," I answered.

By that time a small crowd was standing around me, all looking at my T-shirt. I nodded politely and made a hasty retreat out to my Jeep.

Forty-five minutes later I pulled into the driveway of a nondescript two-story building, covered in robin's egg blue vinyl siding. I met Randy and we walked up a claustrophobic stairway to the second floor.

At the top of the stairs we were met by Sam and his roommate, who showed us around the small apartment. I prefer to have everyone who lives in a residence present when I'm there for interviews and to answer any questions. By having all occupants of a home present, I get everyone's perspective about the paranormal activity occurring in the location.

In addition, nothing is lost in translation when I explain the hows, whys, and reasons a ghost or spirit, if one is present, is behaving the way it is, and what we can do to assist the living and the dead to resolve the situation. In other words, everyone is on the same page.

A kitchen lay to our left, the living room to our right, and the bedrooms lay straight ahead and bordered the living room. Sam's bedroom was the first bedroom.

I took my time and walked around the apartment in an attempt to adjust to the energy and see what spirits, if any, were present. The energy felt statically charged and heavy.

The apartment was a typical bachelor pad: clothes were strewn around and laundry was piled up in the laundry room. Various beer cans, half-filled glasses, and empty pizza boxes littered the coffee table in the living room—the remnants of another good party I hadn't been invited to.

Randy followed me around with the video recorder, and Sam sat on the couch watching me, his big blue eyes filled with the hope that I could extract him from his ghostly situation.

Satisfied there weren't any spirits in the other rooms of the apartment, I turned my attention to Sam's bedroom.

It took my eyes a minute to adjust to the darker room. Heavy curtains blocked out what little light was available, due to the thunderstorms raging outside.

The large room was lit by a lone lamp that cast eerie shadows around the bedroom. Sam turned on another light, further illuminating the room. The walls were barren, but I could see nail holes and tape marks where the pictures and posters, now on the floor or leaning against the walls once hung.

A couch sat against the back wall next to the closet, a queen sized bed rested on the wall to my right, and a large, standing oval mirror stood in the right corner.

I walked toward the mirror and examined it closely; it looked to be an antique.

"That was the only thing in the apartment when we moved in," Sam offered. "We were told by the landlord to not move the mirror or get rid of it."

"Did your landlord say why?" I asked.

"No. I asked, but he wouldn't answer," Sam sighed, sitting on the edge of his bed. "All he would say is that there was a spirit named Zack in the apartment, but he was harmless. I wasn't thrilled, but the rent was cheap and it's close to my job and my church."

"Interesting," I murmured. "So the thought of living with a ghost didn't scare you?"

"Not really. At the time I thought it would be kind of a novelty," Sam said, blushing slightly. "I never imagined it would turn into such a nightmare."

"I'm sure," I smiled. "How does the landlord know the ghost is named Zack?"

"I don't know," Sam shrugged.

"So, Zack is the one who pulled the pictures and posters off the wall?" I asked, turning around to look at Sam.

"Yes. See the empty shelves?" Sam said, pointing to three shelves above his bed. "I had my baseball trophies and other stuff on them, but they would keep falling off and hitting me while I was sleeping. At first I thought the shelves weren't level, but they are. I checked. Plus the stuff would fly off of them and land all over the bed. There was force behind them."

"I see," I answered, looking around the room and noticing the trophies standing in the corner.

Randy sat the video recorder down on top of the dresser by the bedroom door and climbed up on the bed to examine the shelves. He grabbed them and tugged on them, but they didn't budge.

He then retrieved a baseball from the floor and sat it on the shelves one at a time, but the baseball didn't move an inch.

"The shelves seem level." Randy said, satisfied with the results of his test.

Taking my time, I examined every corner of the room, pausing now and then to feel the energy, but the room seemed clear, until I arrived at the mirror. Then the energy changed and became charged with electricity. Something was definitely trying to get my attention; now I just had to figure out who or what it was.

Normally I would just communicate telepathically with a ghost or spirit, but because Randy was video-taping I decided to use a pendulum. I took the rosary from around my neck, kissed the cross, and then let the rosary dangle from my index finger.

"Okay, Zack," I said aloud. "This is how it's going to work: I want you to swing the rosary back and forth for yes, and in circles for no. Do you understand?"

The rosary immediately started to swing back and forth rapidly.

"Okay, good," I said. "Zack, my name is Debi and I'm here to help you. Understand?"

Again the rosary swung back and forth quickly. I stopped it with my hand.

"Excellent. Do you mean anyone here any harm?" I asked.

The rosary rotated in a circular motion. Sam and Randy stood spellbound by the spirit communication taking place.

"Great. Thanks, Zack," I said, again stopping the pendulum from moving. "Are you trapped here?"

The rosary swung back and forth for yes.

"Do you need me to help you go into the light?"

Zack responded by making the rosary swing back and forth quickly.

"Okay, great. Zack, I'm going to move around in the corner of the room by this mirror. When I'm close to you, I want you to make the rosary move toward you. Understand?"

Again, yes.

Holding the rosary in front of me, I slowly moved toward the mirror. When I got about six inches away, the cross jerked violently toward the mirror, repeatedly banging the glass in an excited motion.

Randy and I exchanged quizzical glances; why was the cross hitting the mirror?

Perplexed, I backed up and again walked toward the mirror, and the cross dangling from the rosary repeated the same action.

"Zack," I paused, almost afraid to ask the obvious, "are you trapped inside the mirror?"

The rosary swung back and forth wildly in excitement.

I knew that mirrors could act as portals between the earthly plane and the other side, but I wasn't aware that a ghost or spirit could become trapped in a mirror.

"Okay, Zack. Hang tight and I'll get you out of there," I promised. "Randy, can I talk to you for a minute in the other room?"

Randy switched off his video camera and followed me into the living room.

"So, what's the plan?" Randy asked when we were safely out of Sam's earshot.

"I don't know," I shrugged. "I've never had a ghost trapped in a mirror before. I mean, I've heard of it in theory, just never ran into one."

"Right, mirrors can act as portals between this world and the other side, but how could a spirit get trapped in the mirror? I mean, just come through the portal, right?" Randy asked.

"You would think," I shrugged. "Quite frankly the only explanation I can come up with regarding how Zack got trapped is that the portal closed before he got through, or someone intentionally sealed him in the mirror through some kind of magic."

"Okay...so what are you going to do?" Randy looked at me expectantly.

"I'm going to try to draw him out of the mirror, I guess," I said.

"And what if that doesn't work? What's Plan B?" Randy asked.

"There isn't a Plan B," I answered, walking away from him and back into Sam's bedroom.

Randy sighed heavily and followed behind me, pausing only long enough to switch on his video recorder.

Having to totally focus on the task at hand, I decided to forgo the rosary to communicate with Zack, and have him communicate with me through telepathy. It required less energy for Zack to talk to me telepathically, and he would need all the energy he could get if this was going to be effective.

"Okay, Zack," I said aloud. "This is the deal. You need to communicate with me telepathically—it will help save your energy. I'm going to get you out of that mirror, but you have to promise me one thing."

"What?" I heard Zack say.

"You have to promise me that you will go directly into the light and not hang around here or anywhere else. Okay?" I said.

"I promise. Please help me," Zack pleaded, desperation filling his voice.

"Okay, this is how it's going to work, Zack. I'm going to put my hands on the mirror and force my energy into the mirror. When you feel that energy, I want you to follow it and come out of the mirror through me, then you must leave my body the second you are free. Agreed?" I said. I knew this was a risky move, but I didn't know any other way to get this poor ghost out of the mirror.

"Agreed, I'm ready." Zack answered.

It's not very often that I open myself up in this manner when dealing with spirits. The main reason is that some spirits can pretend to be one thing, when in reality they are something totally different. For example, a demon can take the shape of a child spirit or a loved one who's passed away, in order to gain your trust.

While I was really quite hesitant to do what had to be done, there really wasn't any other way that I knew of to get Zack out of the mirror. I had to take extra precautions to protect myself and keep myself grounded. In addition, I was stalling for time to figure out what I was going to do if Zack didn't hold up his end of the bargain.

After taking a deep breath to ground and center myself, I placed the palms of my hands on the mirror, allowing my energy to flow freely from me and into the mirror.

Almost instantly, I felt Zack's energy begin to merge with mine. My hands started to tingle and the feeling swept rapidly up my arms and soon engulfed my entire body. Within just a few seconds, I felt Zack's energy leave my body and felt him standing next to me.

"Do you see the light, Zack?" I asked.

"Yes, I see it. There aren't words to even begin to thank you," he said.

"You're welcome, Zack. Go in peace," I said quietly.

"I see my family!" Zack exclaimed. With those words, I felt his energy completely leave the room.

"He's gone into the light," I told Randy and Sam, who were looking at me expectantly.

"Will he come back?" Sam asked.

"No, he won't come back," I promised. "Now, it's time to clean house."

I walked out of the bedroom and over to my briefcase, which I'd set on the kitchen table. I extracted a smudge stick and my bottle of holy water.

After lighting the smudge stick, made of white sage, sweet grass, and frankincense, I walked around the entire apartment making sure the smoke from the smudge stick got into every nook and cranny. As I smudged the area, in a calm but assertive voice I ordered any negative energies or spirits to leave immediately.

Once I finished smudging, I opened the holy water and systematically made my way through the apartment. I kept dipping my index finger into the holy water and making the sign of the cross on every window frame, jamb, and door I could find in the apartment.

As I worked, I commanded that any type of ghost or entity leave the space in the name of God. I could feel the energy in the rooms begin to lighten and feel less heavy.

"The house is clean. You should have no more trouble," I announced to Sam.

I could see his jaw unclench, and the features on his face visibly relax.

"Thank you," Sam said.

"You're welcome. If you have any more trouble just let Randy know and we'll come back out," I assured him.

A few minutes later Randy and I packed up our gear and left Sam's apartment.

It's been well over a year, and Sam is still reporting that since we were there, all paranormal activity in the apartment has stopped.

The above story is one of the most interesting of my career as a medium and ghost hunter. It is one of those cases that will stick with me throughout my life— not because it was especially complicated, but because to find a spirit trapped in a mirror, to me, is extremely rare.

It wasn't until Zack was already gone that I thought to ask him how he got trapped in the mirror in the first place, but it's too late now. Zack is exactly where he's supposed to be, and I can only imagine his anguish at being trapped in that mirror.

As I made my way home through the pouring rain, I thought about what just transpired. The entire case made perfect sense now—Zack wasn't being destructive or malicious in his behavior toward Sam; he was simply desperately trying to get someone's attention so he could be helped.

This case is a lesson—not just to paranormal investigators, but to everyone. Just because a ghost or spirit is acting in what you perceive to be a destructive way, it may only be the way some poor soul is crying out in desperation for assistance.

In retrospect, I wonder what would have happened to Sam and Zack if there wasn't a psychic medium present to assist in the situation.

I suppose through a series of electronic voice phenomena, or EVP, sessions it would be possible for an experienced paranormal investigation team to figure out what was going on, but that process could be lengthy, time consuming, and in some cases, unsuccessful.

While I understand many people don't necessarily believe in psychic mediums—and many ghost hunting teams don't use them or use them sparingly because they may believe a psychic medium takes away from the legitimacy of the team—I can't stress enough how sometimes using a psychic medium in an investigation can be efficient and, in some circumstances, more productive than not.

Many people who are experiencing paranormal activity in their homes or places of business don't have any idea how to find a reputable psychic medium to help them with their problem. The best advice I can give on that topic is to find a trustworthy paranormal investigation team in your area, and ask them if they use psychic mediums as one of the tools in their arsenal when conducting an investigation of a possible haunting.

If you do this, don't be afraid to ask for references, and please check out every reference they give you. If a paranormal investigation team will not give you references, then find another team.

Now before I get hate mail from paranormal teams who don't release references due to client confidentiality, I get it, but at the end of a successful investigation, you should ask your client if you can use them as a reference for any potential clients—and get their approval in writing.

The most important thing to remember about this story is that sometimes not everything is as it appears when a ghost, spirit, or other type of entity is present. Every ghost, every spirit, every case is unique and different in its own way. Take nothing at face value.

Chapter 2

NATHANIAL

Sometimes children have imaginary friends, and sometimes their friends are not so imaginary—they're spirits. It's not unusual for children to see ghosts and spirits more than many adults do, because children are more open to their environment than adults are.

As people get older, unless they are psychic, they learn to filter out certain things, which pretty soon becomes second nature, and they become closed off to things they are told are impossible or don't exist. Children, especially small children, haven't learned how to do this, so they are more accepting of everything around them—even if that something is a ghost.

Unless a child is frightened by a ghost or spirit, they will accept them for who and what they are as a natural part of life, which spirits are.

Fortunately, or unfortunately, depending on your individual point of view, I was born a psychic medium and, until the age of seven, assumed everybody could see ghosts. I couldn't have been more wrong, but that's another story.

I met Nathanial when I was at the tender age of five. He lived on the second floor of my great-aunt's house, which contained two bedrooms and deep, winding closets that I was convinced held mysterious, wonderful things. Since my great-aunt only occupied the first floor of the house, the second floor was used mainly for storing long-forgotten antiques, books, furniture, and other items generally reserved for an attic. It was the perfect place for a ghost—and a curious child.

My parents were out of town for the weekend so, as usual, I was left with Great-Aunt Tote, a wonderful woman whom I loved as much as life itself. She laid down to take a nap, after making me promise I wouldn't leave the house, which left me free to explore the second floor.

I made my way up the steep staircase and turned the corner at the landing to walk down the hallway. On my right was a huge bedroom that held boxes of books, furniture, and scads of other items just begging for me to investigate them.

Sitting cross-legged on the floor, I was eagerly emptying out a box when I felt someone enter the room. I looked up and saw the figure of a young man, not any older than eighteen, dressed in old-fashioned britches, suspenders, and a billowy white shirt. His dark hair was shaggy and mussed, and his keen eyes darted around the room nervously. In retrospect, I realize that he looked like someone out of the television show *Little House on the Prairie*. Yet, something seemed off about this man—something was not quite right. I could see through him into the hallway!

"Who are you?" I asked, looking at him with childlike wonder.

"I'm Nathanial," he answered. Yet he didn't speak the words, they just popped into my head.

"Hi, Nathanial, you're a ghost," I said as a matter of fact. I was so used to seeing ghosts practically everywhere I went and sometimes had a hard time distinguishing the living from the dead, but the fact that this spirit was so close to me that I could see through him left me with no doubt about what he was.

Ghosts never scared me, so the presence of another one did nothing to rattle my five-year-old nerves. I have to admit though, that because this was the first time a ghost communicated with me, I was thrilled.

"Yes. But please don't be afraid of me. I'm so lonely," Nathanial pleaded.

"I'm not scared of you," I assured him. "I get kind of lonely, too. We can be friends!"

And so began several years of a unique friendship. When I was at my great-aunt's house, I spent countless hours in the attic with Nathanial. He'd watch me while I colored, played, and explored the treasures hidden in the rooms. We shared secrets, like most children do, but mostly we kept each other company. I told him about what I'd done that week in school or with my friends, and he always listened with rapt attention.

Time marched on, and as I got older my trips to the second floor became less frequent. Eventually my great-aunt died and my dad sold her house. Even though I was no longer able to talk to Nathanial, I thought about him often throughout the years, and I missed him horribly.

About two months before I got married, the people who bought my great-aunt's house called my dad and said they were divorcing, and they asked if he would like to buy the house back.

My dad jumped at the chance, and then sold it to my husband and me for a paltry sum. I couldn't believe my good fortune! I'd be reunited with Nathanial. I'd learned so much about ghosts over the years and now knew that Nathanial belonged in the light, and I had to figure out a way to cross him over to the other side. No matter what, I had to help my first best friend and confidant.

Having Nathanial and two other ghostly occupants complicated things a bit, because I needed to explain to my husband exactly what I was and what I could do. While I'd told him about my abilities when we were dating, I doubt he believed me or took me seriously, but this time he was going to have to—he didn't have any other choice.

I did, however, take the time to go up to the second floor and reacquaint myself with Nathanial. Just as I did when I was a child, I crept up the stairs to the second floor. As I turned the corner to walk down the stairway, I was immediately engulfed by a white mist and what felt like arms wrapping tightly around my body.

"I'm happy to see you, too, Nathanial," I laughed. "Please let me go so we can talk."

The white mist backed away from me and materialized into the Nathanial I remembered. It was then that I realized that Nathanial was mentally challenged. I had a cousin who was mentally challenged and recognized the oversized head, clumsy movements, and other symptoms of the disability. Nathanial cringed when he realized I knew about his disability.

"Now that you know, you won't talk to me anymore," he said telepathically, with profound resignation.

"That's not true. You're my friend and that's all that matters," I said. "When did you die?" I settled myself cross-legged on the floor of the hallway.

"1853, I think," he responded tentatively.

"I don't remember anyone in our family history who had your illness, with the exception of my cousin. Are you a member of my family?" I asked.

"No. I came to this house a long time ago," Nathanial answered, and drifted off into the bedroom to the right of me.

I got up off the floor and followed him. He moved toward the tall, narrow window in the room that looked out the side of the house.

"I used to live over there," Nathanial said.

"Over where?" I asked, joining him at the window.

"On the corner. They destroyed my house to put up another building. I didn't like it there so I came here because the attic was empty," he answered.

"Where the gas station is?" I asked, knowing it was the only building not original to the area at the time Nathanial would have been alive.

"I guess."

"Nathanial, this isn't an attic. It's the second floor to a house. This room is a bedroom. Why do you think it's an attic?" I said.

"My family was afraid and ashamed of me because I was sick, so when we had company, or they didn't want to deal with me, they made me go up to the attic so no one would see me," Nathanial said sadly.

"I'm sorry they did that to you," I said, knowing that what he experienced was customary at the time. "So why haven't you gone into the light and crossed over?"

"Everyone laughed at me and made fun of me when I was alive. It was terrible. I just don't want to go through that anymore. That's why I came here. No one could see me and I wouldn't be laughed at. When you were a little girl you never made me feel different. I'm happy here, now that you're back," Nathanial answered.

"I understand, but if you go into the light, you will be healed. No one will laugh at you anymore, and you can see your family again," I said.

"I don't want to see my family," he said, his energy filled with anger. "I can't talk to you anymore right now." With that he faded away and I felt his energy was no longer in the room with me. Disappointed, I made my way back down the stairs to the first floor.

I knew from experience that Nathanial wouldn't leave the second floor. The farthest he ever came was to the bottom of the stairway; he would wrap his fingers around the edge of the wall and peek around the corner to see what was going on in the rest of the house.

Days turned into weeks, and weeks into months. I became pregnant and gave birth to my son, and then twenty-two months later to my daughter. Nathanial, while still ever-present, refused to go into the light and quite frankly I was too busy with my children to spend a lot of time trying to convince him it was in his own best interest to do so.

As my son got older and learned how to talk, I'd hear him in his bedroom, which is the same room on the second floor that Nathanial hung out in, talking to someone.

"Who are you talking to?" I asked one night after hearing him having a conversation in his bedroom. I sat down on the edge of my son's bed.

"The man, Mommy. He hides when you come up here because he thinks you're going to be mad," my son told me, his dark brown eyes looking earnestly into mine.

"His name's Nathanial," I told my son. "I used to play with him when I was a little girl."

"You did?" His eyes grew wide.

"Yes, and I won't be mad. He doesn't have to disappear when I come up here," I assured him.

"Is he a ghost?" my son asked.

"Yes, he is. But he's a good ghost and won't hurt you," I said.

"Like Casper?"

"Yes," I laughed. "Just like Casper. Now go to sleep."

I tucked my son into bed and walked slowly down the stairs to the first floor. I have to admit I was a little shaken and proud that my son inherited my gift and could see spirits and wasn't afraid of them. But I also knew that I would have to start to teach him the difference between a good ghost and a bad ghost.

With a heavy sigh I sat down on the couch in the living room to think. It's hard enough to be a child without having the added burden of being able to see and talk to the dead. I had to figure out a way to help my child understand the spirit world and accept his gift.

One weekend, my husband decided to hang shelves in my son's room to hold his ever-growing collection of toys and treasures. I told him not to hang the shelves on the wall by the window, because that's where Nathanial liked to stand and gaze out at the place his house used to occupy.

My husband, an engineer who does not entirely believe in my abilities, of course ignored my pleas and hung the shelves with molly bolts right next to Nathanial's window, and made my son climb the shelves, much against my pro-testations, to make sure they were strong and sturdy.

———

A week later my husband and I took the children camping. Upon arriving home late Sunday afternoon, my son raced up the stairs to his bedroom.

"Mom! Come up here!" he cried.

Hearing the fear in his voice, I ran up the stairs and into his bedroom. There I found that the shelves had been ripped from the wall, molly bolts and all, leaving gaping holes in the drywall. It was apparent that the shelves had been thrown violently across the room, leaving the toys scattered everywhere.

I called my husband upstairs and he stood open-mouthed, gaping at the destruction.

"I told you not to hang the shelves there," I said, as I started to pick up the toys and pile them in one of the corners of the bedroom.

"Well, yeah, but I never thought..." My husband's sentence trailed off, left unfinished.

"You really made Nathanial mad, Dad," my son said, trying to hide the smile that played around his mouth.

"I guess I did. We won't make the same mistake this time," my husband answered as he picked the shelves up off the floor and stacked them neatly against a wall far away from the window. I could tell he was trying to hide the shock and fear he felt due to Nathanial's temper tantrum.

We cleaned up the bedroom and my husband rehung the shelves on the opposite wall from the window, leaving Nathanial more than ample space to resume his window gazing. The next weekend my husband patched the holes in the wall by the window and gave the wall a fresh coat of paint, although he insisted that I remain upstairs with him the entire time, in case Nathanial showed up. I never told my husband, but Nathanial was standing at the doorway of the bedroom the entire time, keeping a close eye on the repairs and to ensure that his coveted place by the window wouldn't be impeded.

A few weeks later my parents, who'd come up from Florida for a visit, took the kids with them to visit relatives who lived up north. They would be gone for a few days and I decided this was the best time to try, once again, to get Nathanial to go into the light and cross over to the other side.

I went upstairs to my son's room and sat down on his bed.

"Nathanial, come talk to me," I said. "I'm not mad about the shelves and you're not in trouble."

Within a few seconds Nathanial appeared at the doorway and immediately made his way to the window, gazing longingly toward the lot where his house once sat.

"I'm sorry for what I did," he said. "I didn't mean to scare your children."

"You didn't," I assured him. "But you really need to go into the light, Nathanial. You don't belong here."

"I told you I don't want to see my family," Nathanial said, anger rising up in his voice.

"I understand that. I really do. But it's for your own good. Have I ever lied to you, Nathanial?" I asked.

"No."

"Then you know I'm not lying when I tell you that if you go into the light, you will be healed. You will be healthy, just like everyone else, and no one will make fun of you or be mean to you. You will be happier there," I pleaded.

"I'm scared," he said, turning away from the window to look at me.

From the bottom of my heart, I wished I could wrap my arms around him and give him a hug in an attempt to comfort him, but words were the only tool at my disposal.

"I know you are, honey. It's okay to be afraid. Would it be okay if I got a friend or two of mine from the other side to come help you? They can tell you what it's like over there, something I can't do," I said.

"I will talk to them," Nathanial consented.

"That's all I ask," I told him as I got up from the bed and went to stand beside him at the window. "It will be okay, Nathanial. I promise."

I went downstairs and lay down on my bed, allowing my mind to clear and calling out to my spirit guides. Within a few moments, I felt a ghostly presence enter the room and telepathically, I told my guide that I needed help in getting Nathanial into the light and over to the other side where he belonged.

My guide assented, and assured me that the matter would be handled in a loving and caring manner.

I swear I should have installed a revolving door to the other side in my son's room for the next few days. Spirits were popping in and out so fast, and with such frequency, that it made me dizzy because of all the different energies. Apparently my spirit guides felt it necessary to bring in other spirits to help reassure Nathanial, and help him make the transition to the other side. However, the other two spirits in the house didn't cross over, probably because when they died they crossed over, and chose to come back from time to time to check on things.

The day before my children came home from their trip with my parents, I went upstairs to see how things were progressing with Nathanial. I wandered from room to room in search of him, but to no avail. Nathanial was gone—he'd finally made the transition into the light. The house suddenly felt empty, as if a hole opened up in the energy of the house, and the void I felt in my soul was painful. While I was relieved that Nathanial went into the light, I desperately missed my friend, but it was for the best.

You'd think the story ends there, but it doesn't. A few years after Nathanial left, we sold the house and bought another house a mile or so away.

The day of the move, I was the last one in the house and walked around to make sure nothing was left behind. I went upstairs and wandered through the empty room my daughter once occupied and when I turned around to leave, Nathanial appeared in the doorway. He appeared strong and robust.

"Nathanial!" I said. "What are you doing here?"

"I just came to say goodbye, and to thank you. I'm so happy now that I am where I belong. You have always been my best friend in the world, and I will be there to greet you many years from now when it's your time to cross over."

"You're welcome, my friend," I said, tears welling up in my eyes. "I'm so glad you're happy. I miss you and love you."

"I love you, too. I will never be far away," he answered.

Nathanial's energy faded, and once again I was left alone with my thoughts and emotions.

I took one last look around and walked out of the house, closing the door on that chapter of my life.

I didn't think about it at the time all this was going on, probably because I was so busy with the move and the kids, but since writing this book I've had time to reflect on my experiences with Nathanial. It dawned on me that I really don't recall the other two spirits in the house, who will be discussed in greater detail in the next story, interacting with Nathanial in any way.

However, it's entirely possible that they did interact and Nathanial never mentioned it. This wouldn't surprise me, because Nathanial spoke very little about his existence as a ghost, and it never dawned on me to ask him about it. I'd assumed that ghosts were not uncommon and they existed just like the living do.

It's also possible that all of the ghosts in the house weren't really aware of one another's existence, and so they wouldn't communicate with one another. This could explain why the other ghosts in the house, who obviously had crossed over and chose to return from time to time, didn't leave when Nathanial did, nor try to convince him to cross over.

Just as in the world of the living, in the world of ghosts there are differences between them. For example, some ghosts are earthbound, meaning that they never crossed over to the other side, and some ghosts have crossed over, but have chosen to return from time to time.

There are reasons a ghost might be earthbound, just as there are reasons a ghost has chosen to return. In the case of an earthbound ghost, they may have died suddenly in an accident. They could also have died in their sleep or had a heart attack so severe that death would have been instantaneous. In the previous example the person might not even realize they're dead, because death was so fast.

In the case of Nathanial, he was afraid to cross over because of his life experiences, and who can blame him? I've also run into earthbound ghosts who wouldn't cross over because of their fear of being judged by a higher power, for things they'd done when they were alive.

Spirits that have crossed over may return from time to time to check up on family, deliver a message, or to visit places they loved so dearly in life. These spirits may also show up for special events like weddings, birthdays, the birth of a child by a member of their family that is still alive, or in some cases, they come back to help a loved one who is going through a difficult time in their life. There is a multitude of reasons a spirit who has crossed over may choose to return, even if only for a brief amount of time. It really depends on the spirit and their individual needs, wants, and desires.

Chapter 3

THE ANCESTRAL HOME

As I mentioned in the previous story, Nathanial lived on the second floor of my great-aunt's home. However, Nathanial and my great-grandmother Lillian weren't the only ghostly occupants of that property.

Before we begin to talk about the other ghosts, I believe it's important that you know the history of the property.

Long before land grants were issued for that area of Southfield, Michigan, Native Americans occupied the land, but were forced out by the US government.

My great-grandfather acquired a large parcel of land through the Federal Land-Grant Act, back in the early 1900s. He and my great-grandmother quickly built the house that still stands today and moved in. Shortly after that, my great-grandfather plowed the land and began mushroom farming, along with working in one of the local factories.

Through the years, various members of my family migrated to Michigan, so my great-grandfather converted one of his outbuildings into a comfortable home for the relatives, until they got on their feet in this new area.

Eventually the house moved down the descendant chain, until it became the home of my great-aunt Louisa, affectionately known as Aunt Tote, because when she was a child she liked to be carried or "toted" everywhere.

As I mentioned before, I spent a lot of time at the house with Aunt Tote and Nathanial, although no one but me believed he existed—denial can be a wonderful thing sometimes.

I can remember other spirits being in the house when I was a child, but I didn't pay them any mind, and they pretty much ignored me, as well.

The year I turned fifteen, Aunt Tote became very ill and was close to death. The last time I spoke to her when she was alive she told me, among other things, that when I got married I would have her house. At fifteen, I was nowhere near getting married, but I thanked her politely and after a few more minutes of cherished conversation and goodbyes, she quietly died. I remember sitting by her hospital bed for quite some time, not wanting to believe that she was gone, but once I saw her soul leave her body and ascend into the heavens, I knew I had to let her go. After Aunt Tote's death, my dad sold the house on a land contract to a young couple who'd just been married.

Fast forward five years and I'm not only twenty years old, but I'm months away from my own wedding. My fiancé and I were urgently searching for the perfect place to live, but budgetary restrictions and two totally different tastes in décor were making things difficult.

Two months before the wedding my dad received a call from the people who'd bought Aunt Tote's house; they were getting divorced and wanted to know if my dad wanted to purchase the house back. My dad jumped at the chance, and then sold the house to me. So, in the end, I did have the house when I got married, just like Aunt Tote said I would. However, that was just a hint of what was to come.

What I didn't anticipate is that two other ghosts besides Nathanial were also in the house.

One of the ghosts took a little work to figure out. I hung two pictures in the living room, one over the couch and one over the fireplace. I then ran to the store to get some cleaning supplies. When I returned home, the pictures were reversed, meaning the one over the fireplace was now over the couch and vice versa. I knew no one else was home. My husband was at work and my parents were in Florida. I switched the pictures back where I had originally hung them, and spent the next hour cleaning the kitchen from top to bottom.

When I returned to the living room I found the pictures switched again. *What the hell?* I thought. Then it dawned on me—the pictures were painted by my great-grandmother Lillian, who built the house and lived there for many years.

I called my mom and asked her where Lillian used to have those two pictures hung when she lived in the house. Sure enough, the pictures were hung in the opposite places that I'd hung them; Lillian switched them to where she'd hung them.

After hanging up the phone, I walked into the living room to address Lillian directly.

"Okay, Great-Grandmother. I understand now. I'll leave the pictures where you want them," I said aloud.

While I didn't get any response, I know she heard me because she never bothered those pictures again for the eight years we lived there ... at least until the day came when we decided to sell the house and move to a more family-friendly neighborhood. Not that we lived in a bad area, because we didn't, but the house was on a busy main street and I was concerned about the kids getting hit by one of the speeding cars going by.

After we signed the papers to list the house for sale, my husband left for work and the kids were in school. I'd run a few errands and returned home a couple of hours later, to find one of the pictures Lillian painted on the floor across the room—the glass smashed to smithereens. Apparently she was showing her displeasure that the family home was once again leaving the family. I cleaned up the glass and packed all of her paintings safely away so they could be rehung with honor at the new house.

Now, I have never figured out the third ghost, besides Nathanial and Lillian, even to this day. I could sense the spirit was that of a man, and his energy was very strong, so this meant he was a powerful spirit. While I kept getting the picture in my head of a large, Native American man, I could never prove that's who he was.

This ghost, whom I named Sam for reasons I don't even know, though I knew full well it wasn't his real name, was really quite active in the house. Sam would change the channels on the television in very rapid succession, spin the swivel chairs in the living room, and quickly turn lights on and off if he wanted your attention, or to be acknowledged in some way. Of course he didn't do all of these at the same time, although I have no doubt he was very capable of doing so, if he so chose to.

At first I felt a little intimidated by his presence because of his intense energy, but I soon learned this phantom was not only helpful, but had a very good sense of humor—depending on your point of view, I suppose.

Whenever my girlfriend Sally came over to visit and went to use the restroom, this spirit would lock her in the bathroom. Now this was impossible for a human to do, because the bathroom door didn't have a lock on it. But this spirit would hold the door shut, so Sally couldn't get out.

She would push and I would pull on the door, but it wouldn't budge no matter what we tried. I had to ask the spirit, between hysterical fits of laughter, to let Sally out of the bathroom. Then the ghost would release the door and let my poor, scared friend out of the bathroom.

While I found it particularly hilarious (I know, I'm bad), Sally did not, and would get quite a scare.

No one else would ever get locked in the bathroom except for Sally, and I'm still not sure why this ghost chose to pick on her. The only thing I can come up with is that he knew it would scare her and that's why he did it. I guess even ghosts need to have a little bit of fun every now and then.

Sam also never pulled off any of his antics when the children were awake—only when they were asleep. I guess he didn't want to scare them, which I greatly appreciated. Nor did he really do anything when my husband was home. That may have been out of respect, or because Sam knew my husband wouldn't appreciate his not-so-subtle humor.

Sam also wouldn't communicate with me to tell me who he was or why he was there. I found this to be extremely frustrating, because I felt I had a right to know who was in my own home—even if it was a ghost.

It took a little bit of adjustment, but Sam and our family learned to co-exist. In fact, I came to rely on Sam for little things, like turning on lights if I'd been out and came home to a dark house.

I remember one night when the kids were with my parents, my husband was at work, and I'd gone to the grocery store. When I came home I had my arms full of groceries, and when I got in the house I realized I hadn't turned on any lights— I hadn't expected to be gone so long after dropping off the kids.

I yelled out to Sam to please turn on a light, so I could make my way to the kitchen to set down the groceries.

I was actually quite surprised that Sam turned on the foyer light, one of the living room lights, the dining room light, and the kitchen light. What he'd done was basically light a pathway for me from the front door to the kitchen.

After putting down the groceries, I thanked Sam, finished unloading the car, and began to put away the food. Apparently I forgot to lock the house up, because I heard the decisive click of the lock as the deadbolt slid into place on the front door. I walked out of the kitchen to see if my husband had come home early, but there was no one but me in the house.

One night, however, Sam's normal antics stopped, and took a very serious turn. The kids were in bed, as were my husband and I. In the middle of the night, I was awakened by someone shaking me violently.

I woke up with a start, thinking it was my husband waking me up for some reason, but he lay sound asleep next to me. The house was deathly quiet, and I got out of bed to go check on the children. It was then I noticed that the house was very cold.

I checked the thermostat, which said the house was down to fifty-five degrees. As it was the middle of winter, the house should have been a lot warmer. I woke up my husband and told him the problem.

He ran down to the basement to check the old oil burning furnace and discovered it wasn't working. He then turned off the oil supply to the furnace. We called around and found a twenty-four hour furnace service that dispatched a repairman to our house.

After a careful inspection, the repairman told us that the furnace was shot and we'd need a new one installed in the morning. Then he told us that if I hadn't woken up and discovered the problem, and my husband hadn't turned off the oil supply to the furnace, that the house could have exploded. Sam saved my family's lives that night, by shaking me awake, and I shall always be grateful to him.

The day after we moved out of that house, I drove by it on my way to pick the kids up from school. I noticed that the gutter on the right side of the house had been torn away and grotesquely twisted. It wasn't like that the day before. Perhaps the ghosts were protesting my leaving.

The people who bought the house were well aware that the house was haunted, because they'd asked and I'd told them the truth. They lived in the house only for a short time, while their new house was being built. After they moved out they kept the house as a rental property.

I find it very curious that none of the tenants have lived there more than a year, and most of them must have broken their lease and moved out a lot sooner. Perhaps the ghosts are just too much for them to deal with. Kind of makes you smile, doesn't it?

Chapter 4

THE SCREAMING LADY

When I was contemplating which stories to include in this book, I knew I couldn't leave the story of the Screaming Lady out, because the message is so valuable—it is one of undying devotion, with a healthy dose of desperation thrown in for good measure. Her story teaches us that love transcends death, and persistence can eventually reap huge dividends. It's also one of my favorite ghost stories to date.

I first heard the story of the Screaming Lady from a friend who lived in the state this event occurred. It caught my interest so much that I conducted some independent research. What follows is the sad story of Sarah Christenson.

Most of the time everything appeared to be relatively normal around the white, 1920s, clapboard farmhouse. Cows grazed in the pastures, chickens strutted around the farmyard, and the old farm dog lay snoozing in the shade of his favorite elm tree.

The crops were planted, tenderly cared for, and then harvested and sent to market. The pole barn was filled with more than enough hay to sustain the farm animals through the winter and the farm was settling down in mid-October for a long winter's nap.

Late in the October afternoons, Jack the farmer would corral, milk, and feed the cattle, tuck the chickens safely into their coop, and bring the dog inside to be fed and to keep him warm during the cooling nights of fall.

Then Jack would build a fire in the old wood stove, have dinner, pack his pipe with fragrant tobacco, and settle down in front of the TV to relax.

Yes, most evenings everything seemed normal except for one night each fall—around midnight—when a heart-wrenching scream would pierce the night and jar everyone within a two mile radius of the farm out of a sound sleep.

People who lived close to the farm would race to their bedroom windows just in time to see the ghostly form of a young woman with long, flowing hair, running away from the farmhouse through what was left of the corn stalks in the field, and then fade away. Life on the farm would then return to normal—until next year when the ghoulish scene would repeat itself—just like it had every year since Sarah Christenson was murdered in the 1920s.

The story goes that Sarah was a pregnant woman whose husband was away on business. Late one October night, a group of transient workers who'd been working on a local farm broke into Sarah's house and brutally murdered her.

When her husband returned from his trip, he found his wife's body. After her funeral, Sarah was buried in the church cemetery, in town.

Ever since then, the anniversary of Sarah's death is marked by her ghost appearing to run from the house screaming. Jack and his wife, Emily, became used to the annual event and never really thought much of it. Although the ghost of the Screaming Lady quickly became a local legend, the town was filled with superstitious people who kept a safe distance from the farm during the month of October.

You would think that would be the end of the story, but it's not.

About ten years ago, Jack sold the land and moved into town to retire. The young couple, Mark and Maggie Douglas, who bought the farm, were from out of town and didn't believe in such things as ghosts, and ignored the warnings about the screaming woman.

The Douglases moved into the house and started to work the land. Like clockwork, Sarah would appear screaming every year in late October, but her once-a-year appearance didn't seem to bother the couple.

After living on the farm for five or six years, the Douglases decided it was time to do some remodeling and update the farmhouse. By this time, the couple had become a family, welcoming two beautiful boys, Jason and Mark Jr., into the household.

The Douglases decided that the huge fireplace and mantel in the living room had to go. The enormous hearth jutted out into the room, and was taking up valuable living space that they so very much needed for their growing family.

One early Saturday morning in mid-May, the young couple started demolition on the fireplace. The work was slow and tedious as they chipped away the mortar and took the fireplace apart, brick by brick. They planned to repurpose the bricks into an outdoor grill, so they were careful not to destroy too many of them.

Some of the bricks on top of the mammoth hearth appeared to be rather loose, so they removed them first. That's when they noticed something wrapped in a blanket under the bricks. They worked quickly to remove more of the bricks, and carefully lifted out the small bundle. When they unwrapped the blanket, they were shocked to discover a tiny human skeleton.

They immediately called the local sheriff and notified him of the found human remains. Within a few minutes, sheriff cars were screaming up to the farmhouse, closely followed by the local doctor, who also acted as the coroner.

The doctor was quickly able to determine that the remains were that of a newborn baby, however the cause of death and length of time the baby laid in the hearth were unclear.

The sheriff spent quite a while asking the shaken couple a lot of questions, and once he was satisfied with the answers, left with the doctor, who took the tiny skeleton with him.

News of the discovery of a baby's skeleton traveled fast, as is so often the case in a small, close-knit farming community. Gossip was running rampant in the town's church the next day, so the doctor exercised his right as coroner and ordered that an inquest be held the following Monday. It'd been well over sixty years since Sarah Christenson was murdered.

On the day of the inquest, there was standing room only inside of the small courtroom. Almost everyone in the small town was in attendance, dressed in their Sunday finery. The ladies wore their best dresses and hats, and the men were dressed in shirts, ties, and their best blue jeans—some men even wore suits for the occasion.

The sound of high heels and cowboy boots against the worn wooden floor of the courthouse did little to drown out the murmur of muted voices as people discussed what the inquest was going to uncover. The mood remained solemn and serious. After all, as far as the townsfolk were concerned, an innocent baby died in a most gruesome way.

The sheriff took his place at the long table that had been set up in front of the elevated judge's bench. He was followed closely by the tall, slim coroner, with his hawkish features and sharp, dark eyes that scanned the crowd.

The town attorney, an older woman with graying hair, stern features, and a heavy build, lumbered into the room and took her place next to her husband, the sheriff. The wooden chair protested loudly under her weight to the point that many people waited to see if the chair would give way, sending the attorney tumbling to the floor.

The judge was the last to enter the room. His black robe billowed out around him as he walked, making him look twice his size. He took his place on the bench and banged his well-used wooden gavel several times to bring the inquest to order. The sheriff was then called upon to give his report.

The sheriff rose from his chair, and with an air of self-importance, related the story from the time he was called to the scene, until the baby's remains were removed from the house.

The coroner then spoke in a clear, sharp voice, and announced that the baby was placed in the hearth some time ago and that no cause of death could be found, due to lack of any tissue left on the baby to run sufficient tests. The lack of information led to a collective gasp and whispering among the crowd of onlookers, who were looking for more definitive answers.

The judge then told the crowd that if anyone had any potentially relevant information regarding this matter that they should come forward now and share what knowledge they had.

Eighty-seven year old William Walters, who'd discreetly taken a seat at the back of the courtroom, watched the proceedings carefully. His wrinkled, weather-worn face crinkled up in thought and his milky blue eyes half-closed as he searched his memory for any possible answers. Then it hit him—he was positive he knew to whom the baby belonged.

Tentatively, he raised his calloused hand and waited patiently for the judge to call him up to the front of the courtroom. As he stood up, he grabbed the back of the seat in front of him for balance, and slowly shuffled his arthritic body toward the front of the room, relying heavily on his cane for support.

A young man jumped up and helped Mr. Walters get settled in a chair in front of the panel, for which he was very grateful.

"I believe the baby belongs to Sarah Christenson, better known as the Screaming Lady," Mr. Walters said, his voice raspy from years of smoking. "As I recall, Mrs. Christenson was pregnant when she was murdered, but no baby was found at the time of her death. How the baby got into the hearth of the fireplace I haven't a clue."

The room instantly became abuzz at this prospect. Most people forgot about the Screaming Lady until October, when her unearthly scream filled the darkest of nights.

"Quiet!" the judge roared as he banged his gavel. The crowd immediately fell silent. "Mr. Walters, I accept your premise, as there seems no other likely scenario. The question is; what do we do with this poor baby?"

Much discussion ensued on the topic, and it was finally decided, thanks to a charitable contribution by the local funeral director, that the casket of Sarah Christenson be exhumed and the baby placed in her arms. Albeit a gruesome prospect, the townspeople agreed unanimously; they were ready to be finished with this tragedy that blemished the town's good reputation in the county.

On a dreary, rainy Saturday morning, Sarah Christenson's body was exhumed. The fragile skeleton of the baby, tenderly wrapped in a soft blanket, was carefully placed in the young woman's arms. The casket was then resealed and returned to its final resting place.

That October, and every year since the baby was returned to the young mother, the Screaming Lady has been silent. She can no longer be seen running through the barren corn field, nor do her heart-breaking screams punch through the darkness.

It's speculated that all Sarah Christenson ever wanted was for someone to find her baby and reunite them. As an earth-bound spirit, she was using the anniversary of her death in an attempt to send a message to anyone who would listen that her baby was missing.

This young mother's love for her unborn child transcended death, and now that they are reunited, there is no longer a reason for her to run screaming through the fields. She and her child are together and at peace for all eternity.

Chapter 5

FRANKLIN'S STORY

Sometimes as a psychic medium, a ghost wanders into your life that is unforgettable and will stay with you all the days of your life, and perhaps even remain with you after death. Franklin's story is haunting—a bit tragic, but in many ways endearing.

Franklin taught me that the personality you carried with you throughout your life doesn't change much after death. In Franklin's case, anyway, any changes that happened after his death were subtle. He had an extremely long time to reflect on his life, and the lives of those around him, and in some ways I think he made peace with himself—something he didn't do before he died. However, his strongest character traits—stubbornness, arrogance, and his sense of entitlement—stayed with him long after his body rotted in the ground. He exists in this plane in spirit form only.

Franklin is an earthbound spirit by choice. He knows he can cross over to the other side any time he chooses; the point is he doesn't choose to. Is he right in his decision? You can be the judge after you read his story.

I met Franklin's ghost in a decaying, pre–Civil War mansion that had been undergoing renovation by the current owners. However, due to divorce, all the renovations had stopped and the mansion, a mere shell of its former self, was once again up for sale.

A friend of mine was close friends with the owners, and I was granted access anytime I wanted to be there—which was almost all the time.

At first, Franklin tried to scare me away by attempting to push me down a staircase, but I'd been warned by a friend who'd been almost shoved down the stairs in that house some months earlier, when she was helping the owners attempt to remodel the house.

I remember creeping up the well-worn stairs, varnished a deep mahogany, and feeling two unseen hands grab my shoulders.

Before the ghost could act any further, I told it to "Back off." The ghost immediately scurried into a dark corner of the third floor of the house.

With time, and a lot of encouragement on my part, I got the ghost of Franklin to trust me, and we became what I would call "friends."

I knew from my research on the property that Franklin was the ghost of the son of the original owner, Robert. I knew that Franklin died in 1887 and assumed, rightly so, that he'd been wandering the halls of the mansion since that time.

The third floor of the mammoth estate, like almost all the other floors, had been demolished down to the studs, and the original wide-planked wood floors, which once were varnished to a high-gloss mahogany shine, now were worn and covered with dirt.

The brick outside walls were barren, and a hole in one of the brick walls revealed the spot where an old fireplace once sat. The long-dead radiators were still set against the walls, and three bleak light bulbs dangled from their wires in the ceiling.

Daylight made a vain attempt at illuminating the rooms through dirty narrow windows, but even on the brightest of days, the third floor seemed dark and foreboding. No matter how warm it was outside, the third floor of the house always held a distinct chill, due to Franklin's presence, and whenever I planned to be there for an extended period of time, I always took a blanket with me.

One rainy morning, I packed up a blanket and thermos of coffee and headed over to the mansion to spend time with Franklin. I could sense he often felt lonely in the place, and obviously, there weren't many people he could talk to since the house was completely empty. The current owners, Jake and Sandy, were living in their own home a few miles away. Knowing the house was haunted, and because of my love of the paranormal, they'd graciously given me a key, so I was free to come and go as I please.

I let myself into the house and climbed two flights of stairs up to the third floor. I settled in by the only remaining inside wall, which butted up against the extremely narrow staircase up to the cupola.

"Franklin, are you here?"

Within a few seconds, the ghost of Franklin appeared next to me. His energy felt excited, so I knew he was happy to see me.

"Tell me your story, Franklin."

He nodded in assent.

I poured myself a cup of hot coffee, and nestled it between my hands to warm them. Franklin's tall, thin frame rose up in ghostly form, and began to pace the hallway leading down the entire length of the third floor. His long, ghostly fingers touched at the tips, forming a pyramid, and he bowed his head for a moment to gather his thoughts.

I could make out his dark Victorian suit, vest, and even the chain on his pocket watch. His hard-soled shoes made no noise as he wafted back and forth in the hallway in front of me.

What follows is Franklin's story, in his own words.

"I've walked among the living for over a hundred years now, although it only seems like yesterday when I was a living, vibrant man.

"I've watched from the shadows as people live out their foolish little lives. Little do they know what comes after death —an eternity of torment and suffering? I've seen my empire crumble into decay around me, knowing I'm powerless to stop it. This must be hell, because no God would allow a soul to suffer as mine has." Franklin's voice turned bitter as he spoke.

"So, have you always lived in Michigan?" I sipped my coffee and snuggled farther under my blanket.

"No." Franklin shook his head. "It all started with my father, the saint, who moved us to this insufferable place."

"Your father was Robert, right?" I interrupted.

"Yes. He built this mansion that has now become my prison. Everybody sang his praises during his life and long after his death. Such a benevolent man, a savior to this small hamlet, they said. 'Remember after the great fire how he rebuilt the town?' they cooed. 'Wasn't it nice of him to leave money in his will to build a school for our children?' This town adored him.

"Bah! I spit on his grave!" Franklin's ghoulish face contorted into an angry mass. "Yes, the great saint gets to go to heaven, and I, the clever and ruthless man in business, am now destined to walk the halls of this house I hated so much for all eternity. Ironic, isn't it? It was I who more than doubled the fortune! It was I who suffered so much in life, and yet in death am I allowed no peace?"

"I've always found that peace is subjective." I shrugged. "Where did you move here from?"

"We moved here from Massachusetts in the late 1850s, because my father saw opportunity. I too saw the opportunities, however they differed greatly from my father's. In retrospect, maybe they were not that much different; we just went about obtaining our goals in different ways.

"My father amassed a fortune and gave back to the people whose backs he broke while climbing the industrial ladder. I simply followed in his footsteps, but I kept the fortune I worked so hard to obtain.

"I went to law school and studied hard. I knew how important understanding the law was, especially if you intend to shape it to achieve your desires. I spent years working side-by-side with my father. Observing carefully all the deals he made, learning from them, learning how to do them better."

"I understand," I nodded. "You must have found some happiness—you got married."

"Happiness?" Franklin's ghostly laugh echoed off the walls. "There is no such thing as lasting happiness. In a small town people talk, and a man of my standing in the community should be married. I thought to myself one day, it would be good for business.

"A wife is a necessary evil to handle the entertainment for business associates and to exchange gossip with other women of her standing. You never know what you'll learn from gossip if you listen hard enough. So I found an agreeable woman and married her. By this time, my father was becoming ill with arthritis. It became necessary for me to assist him in the various businesses we owned throughout the area. It was a comfort to know that my wife was overseeing the household. One less thing I had to worry about. Over the years she became a valuable asset to me."

"She was a person, Franklin! She had feelings, dreams, and needs," I protested. "She wasn't your property. How sad a life she must have led."

"She lived a good life." Franklin's ghost wheeled around to face me, crouching down so that his ghostly face was inches from mine. "How dare you judge me!" he roared.

"Perhaps you need to be judged! But that's your biggest fear, isn't it, Franklin? To have someone judge you for the actions you took when you walked among the living is your worst nightmare. From all the newspaper accounts I've read, you were quite the bastard in life and no one really mourned your passing. I see that you haven't mellowed much in death." I jumped to my feet and began to gather my things.

"Please don't go," Franklin pleaded. "I'm sorry, it was wrong of me to treat you so rudely in my home. I get so lonely. Please stay."

I resettled myself on the floor and poured myself another cup of coffee. "So tell me about your daughter. Tell me about Betsy." I already knew most of Franklin's family history from doing research at the Historical Society and at the library, but I wanted to hear it from the horse's mouth, so to speak.

Franklin's face softened, and for a moment I thought I saw a spark of life come back into his cold, dead eyes.

"In 1861, my wife bore me a daughter. I'd been hoping for a son, but the girl child was so beautiful and sweet, and in time I forgot the desire for a male heir. When she got older, I saw to it that she attended a finishing school back East. A young woman of her social standing required only the best education and instruction in the social graces.

"I hoped she'd marry well, and I would have a son-in-law who was worthy to take the reins to the empire I'd amassed.

But alas, she fell in love with a man ten years her senior, and a schoolteacher no less! My God, he lived in a boarding house! I was mortified! How could this have happened? I was so careful to see that she met only the right type of gentlemen—men who were worthy of her and capable of running the family business when I retired. Yet, despite my attempts to discourage this unholy union, they married in December of 1880. My daughter could be headstrong at times, and I, being too overindulgent with her, finally acquiesced, although privately I seethed."

"Why? Being a schoolteacher is a noble profession," I interjected.

"Maybe now." Franklin shrugged his shoulders. "But at that time, it wasn't looked upon as being a noteworthy profession."

I nodded in understanding. "Go on."

"In 1870, my father got elected to the state Senate. In 1871, he died. My mother insisted on a funeral fit for a king and a monument to match. It cost a small fortune, but after all, it was my father.

"In his will, he left a large sum of money to the town to build a school. I fought it tooth and nail for two years. The family fortune belongs in the family, dammit! Eventually I lost and ended up giving this godforsaken place even more money.

"He also left a large sum of money to my daughter, who was nine at the time, with me acting as trustee. I invested her money well, and it became a most tidy sum by the time she reached adulthood. Fortunately for me, she had no head for money, and allowed me to manage her estate, even after her marriage.

"Then one day the unspeakable happened. My darling daughter, who'd been married only three months, died. The circumstances surrounding her death I took with me to my grave. Isn't that a joke? My body rests in peace, yet I shall never rest.

"I commissioned a glass coffin to hold her fragile body, and spent a considerable amount of time selecting just the right monument for the grave. I finally decided on using marble for the material, and had it ornately carved into a bed."

"I'm sorry, Franklin. I've been to her grave—it's beautiful," I said.

"Thank you," Franklin said. "Although I did not shed a tear at her funeral, inside I nearly died. I stood in stoic silence as they gently lowered her into the ground and covered her with dirt. My wife and other family members wept openly. I do not condone such public displays of grief, not in this family. We mourn in private and hide the grief from the world outside. After all, we are of high society, and it isn't proper.

"After the funeral, my daughter's husband came to me and told me he wanted the money due to him. He argued that he was married to my precious daughter, and her money was legally his. He wanted to go back to his family and start a new life. I lied and told him some bad investments caused Betsy's estate to suffer. Then I set my plan of action. There was no way I was going to turn this great amount of money over to the man, who was nothing more than a social-climbing weasel!

"A few days later, I had him sign a paper stating he had no further interest in the estate of my daughter, and gave him a check for $2,000—a mere pittance considering the true value of the estate. Then I walked him down to the train station and purchased him a ticket home. I'd already had one of the maids pack his belongings in a worn, tattered suitcase, which he held tightly in his hands, and I sent him on his way.

"I then immersed myself into my work. The only thing I ever held dear to my heart had been taken away. What else was I to do? Then, as some kind of cruel punishment, I was stricken with the same affliction my father suffered from. It wasn't long before I was forced to use the cane, although I feel it made me look like distinguished and dapper. I had several canes custom-made from only the finest materials. They became a symbol of my status and wealth in the community. God, I was a pompous ass!"

I couldn't help but agree with him.

"Soon my illness became such that I was forced into retirement. It was not easy to conduct my business this way, but I managed. I'd been careful to surround myself with good people I could trust and who were loyal. Although I doubt loyalty had much to do with it—most likely it was fear.

"Then, a few years later, I suffered a horrific fall down the stairs and broke my neck. A short time later, I died from those injuries. Correction there, it should be *my body died*; my soul shall reside in this house and on this land forever. No one should ever dare to take what is rightfully mine!

"So I am trapped here, in this crumbling mansion, forced to walk the stairs, hallways, and rooms of this once-glorious estate. I've tried, oh so many times, to force out the living who dared move into my house, and to no avail.

"Then one day, I discovered I had the power to force them out, at least some of them. Others, who were not afraid of me, stayed. I suppose you could say we forged a peaceful alliance, but it would be more accurate to say I lost my will to chase them out. I suppose the company of the living is better than no company all.

"I also discovered, quite by accident one day as I was roaming the barren rooms, that my daughter's soul came to the house from time to time. It was as though she didn't want me to be too lonely. Bless her heart.

"Yet, in time, her visits became more infrequent. She enjoyed the company of the living, and would leave each time the house became vacant. Perhaps she couldn't stand the silence.

"During one of her stays at the estate, we discussed her death and my act of vengeance toward her husband. She chastised me greatly. I feel no regret for my actions. They were perfectly justified, but she fails to understand my reasoning.

"She forbade me from telling anyone how she died—like I could anyway—at least until you came along. She said it was her story to tell, and when the time was right she would tell it. Her reasoning is beyond me, but I must respect her wishes."

I heaved a deep sigh of disappointment. One of the greatest mysteries of the town was how Betsy died, and it was painfully clear I wasn't going to get any closer to knowing the truth. "So the real reason you're still here is to protect the family secrets, and not the fear of judgment as you proclaimed earlier?" I provoked.

"Someone has to!" Franklin wheeled around to face me, his phantom face twisted in anger. "Don't you see how important our family is? Don't you realize the humiliation we would suffer in our social circle if the truth came out?"

"Franklin, you've been dead over 150 years! No one really cares anymore except for a precious few, whose only real question is how Betsy died. Everyone else is dead! You don't even come up in conversation!" I jumped to my feet so I could meet him eye to eye.

We stared each other down for what felt like hours, but in reality was only just seconds. Then, without another word, Franklin vanished.

"You get back here!" My words echoed throughout the cavernous third floor. I'd never had such a vicious argument with a ghost before, and I wasn't sure what was going to happen. Perhaps I'd pushed Franklin just a little too far. Sometimes, when dealing with a ghost, such a harsh dose of reality can do more harm than good.

I sat back down on the cold, hard floor and poured myself another cup of coffee out of my thermos. I took a sip, allowing the hot liquid to warm me from the inside out.

Within a few moments, Franklin once again appeared before me. "I apologize for my behavior," he said.

"Forgiven. I'm sorry too. I should have never spoken to you that way."

"I deserved it. Now, where were we?" Franklin's translucent figure settled down on the floor across from me.

"Why don't we change the subject, since we appear to be at an impasse? Tell me about your existence since you died," I said.

"Well." Franklin raised a ghostly hand and stroked his chin. "For the longest time I was confused. I really didn't realize I died. I couldn't figure out why everything was gone and people I didn't know were in my house. I couldn't affect my environment at all, and I became extremely frustrated."

"Understandable." I nodded.

"I tried to talk to the people, but they behaved as if they couldn't see or hear me. That's when I realized I was deceased. Naturally, it took me awhile to come to terms with my own death, and I retreated to the cupola—up the staircase behind you. No one alive ever went up there, so I figured I was safe, you know?"

"Right," I said.

"One night when I was walking through the house, Betsy showed up and tried to convince me to go with her to heaven, as she called it. But I knew I couldn't follow her. She begged me to follow her and leave, but it was impossible. Someone has to stand watch over the place. I've tried to make her understand, but to this day, I don't think she does.

"Anyway, it took some time, but I learned how, in my own way, to make the living that dared to invade my property aware of my presence. I would stomp up and down the staircase, move their tools when they were working on the house, and when they tried to come up to the third floor, which I now call home, I would try to push them down the stairs—something I'm not proud of, but one must protect one's privacy, don't you agree?"

"Yes, to a point. But you let me come up here to visit with you anytime I wish," I told him.

"True, but you're the first person in over 150 years that understands, and who I can really communicate with." A smile played around his phantom face.

"Which brings me to the point of my visit today, Franklin." I couldn't look into his eyes. "There was a meeting in town last night, and your home is going to be torn down."

"What?!" Franklin leaped to his feet, well, as much as a ghost can do that. "Why?"

"Because the house is in such disrepair and, according to a structural engineer, it can't be fixed," I said. "People were at the meeting who tried to save the house, me included. But there was little we could do. I'm so sorry, Franklin."

"What am I to do? What's going to happen to me? Where can I go?" Franklin's ghost paced frantically up and down the hallway.

"You could join your family on the other side," I suggested.

"Never!" Franklin's voice roared in my head. "I shall stay here and fight!"

"As you wish, Franklin." I rose from my seat and gathered my blanket and thermos. "Godspeed, my friend."

"You won't be back?" Franklin stopped in his tracks. I don't think this fact ever occurred to him.

"No, Franklin. I won't be back. The house will be gone in a few days. There's really no reason for me to come to an empty lot."

Franklin's ghost moved toward me and stopped just short of where I was standing. "I have to admit I'll miss you." He bowed his head.

"I'll miss you, too. Goodbye." I walked slowly down the two flights of stairs to the first floor and let myself out of the house for the last time.

A few days later, the once-glorious mansion was reduced to a pile of rubble and hauled away. I, like many of the towns-folk, gathered at the scene to mourn the death of another historical landmark. We gathered up some bricks from the house as mementos.

A couple of months after Franklin's house was destroyed, I was in the antique store in town, having coffee and donuts with some of the other local women. One of them told us that the man and woman who lived next to the mansion, and who'd fought the hardest to have it destroyed, were having a horrible time with paranormal activity. They'd hear foot-steps, items in their home were being moved, and doors would open and slam violently.

I smiled to myself, knowing that Franklin had found an-other place to live, and I could appreciate the irony of the situation. The people who detested his home the most were now going to have to live with the ghost of Franklin, whom they'd displaced. You just have to love karma.

Chapter 6

THE WEEPING WOMAN

This is one of those stories that just tugs on your heartstrings. After you read it, you won't find it hard to imagine the depth of one woman's grief and devotion to her husband and child. It's one of the saddest ghost stories I've ever run across. Yet in a way, it's inspirational, because it makes you realize just how alike life and death are. Remember, death is not the end, but the beginning of a new life in spirit form.

An abandoned house still stands defiantly on a lonely patch of land, just outside of a small town in rural Iowa, close to where a friend of mine grew up. Fortunately, the history of the house is very well documented.

The house was originally built as a single-room log cabin in 1881 by a preacher, his wife, and their nine children. They hunkered down during the winter, but at the first sign of spring they began to enlarge their cabin to house their large family.

By 1889, the family moved on and the house was taken over by the township for operation as a stagecoach station.

However, the stagecoach stopped running through the rural area in 1893, so the township then turned the building into a boarding house for trappers and people heading toward the Wild West.

According to local legends and various historical documents, this was a dangerous time, and several gangs of outlaws roamed the area. There were also threats from Native American uprisings. Although there was a minor uprising several miles away, the marauding tribe never got as far east as the tiny town, and there isn't any documentation that the Native Americans caused any trouble in the town that I was able to discover.

The building was again abandoned in 1898, and in 1903 it was converted into a schoolhouse for the children of the railroad workers that streamed into the area. The school operated until 1925 when the building was once again abandoned, although it was used by the large number of drifters, vagabonds, and hobos that roamed the area during the Great Depression. The desolate location and natural water supply made it a safe haven for those who'd been dislocated by the Depression and the Dust Bowl.

When the railroad died in the early part of the 1920s, there were already rumors circulating about the building and its ghosts.

In the 1950s, the house was purchased by a local family, who once again turned it into a family home. The family—a farmer, his wife, and children—only lived in the house a year before mysterious happenings in and around the house drove them out and forced them to move into town.

In 1995, the Historical Society purchased the property with the intent of restoring the house as it had been when it was run as a stagecoach station. Everything went well during the first stages of reconstruction.

However, while clearing out the old well, the volunteers uncovered the skeleton of a small infant. It was shortly afterward that the plans to restore the building hit several snags—and of course, there was the matter of the ghosts. From all accounts, the Weeping Woman began appearing more and more often, frequently scaring the workers until they packed up and finally left.

While I'm unclear about what happened to the infant skeleton, I'm very clear about the increase in paranormal activity after the baby was discovered; the mother was there protecting her baby, even though the baby was long dead. One should never underestimate a mother's love and devotion to her child.

After this discovery, there was a half-hearted attempt to restore the old place, but according to the Historical Society, the home was suffering from too many structural problems to be saved. Some people admitted there'd been a lot of strange things going on at the old homestead that no one could, or would, explain.

When I went to Iowa to visit a friend of mine she told me about this house, and I had to investigate. While my friend was at work, I raced out to the house.

The first time I went into the house, I saw an old wicker rocking chair at the top of the stairway. It took me a couple of minutes to realize that it was slowly rocking back and forth. There wasn't even a breath of wind outside, so I knew the rocking wasn't due to natural causes. As I watched, I saw the spirit of a young woman appear in the rocking chair, and she appeared to be holding a baby, who was tightly wrapped in a white blanket. I couldn't see the face of the baby, but could distinctly make out the top of the baby's head. I could also hear the woman softly crying as she slowly rocked back and forth, hence the name, Weeping Woman.

I slowly made my way to the staircase, trying not to startle her. I tested each step under my foot and worked my way slowly up the staircase. I stopped mid-way up the stairs, because the woman rose from the chair and moved across the open loft toward the center bedroom at the far end of the second floor.

I slowly climbed the rest of the way up to the loft, to follow the phantom woman. In retrospect, I should have taken time to inspect the floor of the loft before I ventured farther, but a sagging loft floor was the last thing on my mind. Halfway across the loft, I felt the floorboards give way under me and I fell through the floor.

Somehow, I landed on the old sofa in the living room of the first floor and once I got my bearings, I looked up toward the gaping hole in the floor above me. I gingerly got up off the sofa and, once I was sure I wasn't too seriously hurt, I scampered back up the stairs, but I couldn't see any sign of the ghostly woman and her baby.

It took a bit of research, but I found the woman who now owns the land the old house sits on. When I sat down to talk to her a couple of days later, the first question she asked was as if I'd seen the Weeping Woman. I nodded yes, and asked who she was.

The woman, who wishes to remain anonymous, told me that sometime around the end of the Civil War, a young couple lived in a house that once stood close to the existing structure. While the husband was away fighting the war, the young, pregnant woman was left alone. Just days after the birth of the baby, the young mother received news that her husband had been killed in battle. Now either she smothered the baby, or the baby died of an illness, but according to the story, the baby died and the young mother threw herself out the second story window, with the baby in her arms.

According to legend, the woman didn't die right away, but laid outside the home for a couple of days before her grief and injuries took her life. The woman told me that historical documents exist which verify that the family lived in the house around the time the Civil War ended, but I couldn't verify the circumstances surrounding the death of the woman that lived there during that time.

Another story related to me by the landowner, which is only loosely tied to the house, is about the time the building was being used as a stagecoach stop, and there was a stagecoach coming in from the west.

The stagecoach was ambushed by bandits and all of the passengers aboard were murdered. The stagecoach was found in the clearing across the road from the station the next morning, overturned and in flames.

The bodies of the passengers were found a short distance away, all neatly buried in a ditch. However, in 1981, when an old humpback bridge was taken out and replaced by a series of culverts covered by a concrete bridge, the skeletons of two women and three men were uncovered by the excavation. This discovery bore out the sketchy tale and the bodies were reburied in the local cemetery, on the other side of town, miles from where they'd laid all those years.

There have also been reports about a ghostly Model A Ford that will come careening off the gravel road, and crash upside down in the creek that runs by the home of the Weeping Woman.

No one seems to know where this car came from or who was driving it, but the story is that on an icy winter night, an accident occurred. The car hit the uprights of the wooden humpback bridge at the bottom of the hill, and flipped into the creek.

The bodies of a young couple were found almost a mile downstream a few days later. A small boy of about five years old was found at the same time in the old house. Although the boy lived, thanks to the "nice white lady" that took care of him, he seemed completely traumatized by the ordeal. Eventually he was sent back east to live with relatives.

In recent years, the ghost car has put in several appearances, one night literally running a lumber truck off the road and into the creek. The driver and his assistant were able to bail out of the truck and land in a ditch unhurt, before their runaway truck crashed to a stop in the creek. The men looked, but could find no sign of the old car that ran them off the road.

Efforts to save the old homestead have long been abandoned, due to the paranormal activity and lack of funds. However, there is one brave soul who did build a log house on the other side of the road. It took him five years longer to build than he'd planned, because the site was plagued by one mishap after another.

In 2010, just one year after the house was finished, he went out into the woods and took his own life, for reasons only known to him. A journal kept in his home and located after his death, told a tale of haunted happenings in and around the house across the street. Although no one knows why the man chose to end his life, the speculations run wild, as they do in a small town, and they all lead to the haunted house across the street that is home to the Weeping Woman.

Many years have passed since that day when I first met the Weeping Woman. The house is little more than a pile of rubble now, and the only thing standing is the lower half of the massive fireplace.

The log home across the street is also empty, and the local wildlife has already started to reclaim it.

Although the locals claim that on a quiet, moonlit night, if the wind's blowing just the right way, you can hear the mournful sounds of a young woman weeping, as she rocks back and forth, holding her dead baby.

Given the tragic history of the house, I'm not really surprised at the amount of paranormal activity occurring there.

I believe that most of the activity is residual, meaning there isn't a ghost present, just a period of time replaying itself, over and over like a tape recorder. However, the presence of one or more intelligent entities is not out of the realm of possibility.

Yet, because of the tragedies that have befallen that one parcel of land, one can't rule out the possibility of all that negative energy attracting a demonic entity that would amplify the apparent paranormal activity already occurring there.

Furthermore, it could help explain the suicide of the neighbor across the street. You see, demons need to feed—and they feed on energy—lots of it. Since the home of the Weeping Woman wasn't occupied by a living soul, it would make sense that a demon would search out the closest available living being, so it could feed.

Being in the presence of a demon, or having a demon occupy your home, isn't pleasant by any stretch of the imagination. In fact, it would be downright terrifying and could, given the right set of circumstances, cause a person to commit suicide. While I personally haven't read the contents of the journal that poor man left behind, the fact that, according to local gossip, he wrote about the abundance of paranormal activity in his house and in the home of the Weeping Woman, could substantiate the theory of a demonic entity having a hand in the man's death.

Chapter 7

WHAT'S GOING ON AROUND HERE?

In an area near where I live, on the eastern coast of Michigan, there appears to be an overabundance of concentrated paranormal activity. While I believe some of it is residual energy, meaning there's no ghost present, just a moment in time replaying itself over and over, there are also some intelligent entities that interact with the living. Some of these spirits are simply haunting a place they loved or knew when they were alive, but others, not so much, and there are a few theories as to where they came from and why they are here.

Part of the subdivision that I live in, including my own house, is built on fill dirt, excavated when the state built a freeway many years ago. Some of these displaced spirits may have been tied to the land and came with the fill dirt when it was excavated.

Another possible scenario is that many of these spirits are from an old town that used to be on the shores of Lake

St. Clair and once stood in the same area as the houses do now. The town was flooded out many years ago. A cemetery and remnants of the town have been found underwater, close to the shores of the lake.

Whichever theory you choose to go with, these are their stories.

The Tragic Ghost of Minnie Quay

Among southeastern Michigan paranormal investigators, there are certain stories of hauntings that have become legendary. The ghost of Minnie Quay is one of those stories.

Minnie Quay lived in the town of Forester, which is nestled on the coast of Lake Huron a few miles north of Port Huron, and quite a distance from my own home. When Minnie Quay lived there, Forester was a bustling lumber town and an important shipping port for boats hauling lumber all over the Great Lakes region.

The Quays—James and his wife, Mary Ann—came to Michigan from New England to take advantage of the booming economy during that time, and to raise their daughter, Minnie.

Four warehouses sat by the shore and a long pier extended out into Lake Huron. The townsfolk would rush to the docks every morning to see which ships had come in, and to hear news from other parts of the region.

Like many girls in shipping towns, Minnie fell in love with one of the sailors who visited Forester when his ship was in dock to be loaded or unloaded. No one is exactly sure of the sailor's name, but speculation runs high, as it always does in a small town. Because of the Quay's high status in the community, the relationship was frowned upon, not just by the townsfolk, but by her parents as well.

Finally, unable to reason with the young girl, James and Mary Ann forbade Minnie from seeing the sailor. Thinking this was the end of it, life went on as normal during the long winter, which stopped shipping traffic.

In the early spring of 1876, as the story goes, news reached the town of Forester that the ship Minnie's sailor worked on had been sunk by a terrible storm. There were no survivors.

Minnie was devastated and beside herself with grief. A few days after hearing the news that her beloved man was dead, Minnie committed suicide by walking off the end of the pier into the frigid waters of Lake Huron. Her body was recovered, and she was buried in the Forester Cemetery at the north end of town, but as you can imagine, she is not resting in peace.

It's been said that Minnie's ghost walks along the shores of Lake Huron, crying mournfully as she searches for her lost love, whom she is never able to find. It's also been reported that she stands in the water where the old pier once stood and tries to beckon young women into the water, to join her in her watery death.

There also have been several reports of her being seen in the bar that stands not too far away from the old pier, now nothing more than a few weather-worn pylons reaching out from the waters of Lake Huron, and which stand as a grim reminder of the tragic story of the young girl. Minnie was only fifteen at the time of her death.

The town of Forester is no longer a shipping port and in the winter is practically deserted, all but for a few residents. However, in the summer the area is teaming with campers and vacationers who come to the shores of Lake Huron to fish, boat, and relax.

I have to admit that as fascinated as I am with the ghost of Minnie Quay, I haven't really gone looking for her as of yet. The area where she drowned is now on private property. There is a house in Forrester that has a plaque marked "Quay," and many people believe this is where she lived, but a local told me that's not the original home of Minnie Quay.

Every summer, tourists will flock to the area to camp and enjoy Lake Huron. As they sit around the campfire late at night, they will tell the story of Minnie Quay and keep her legend alive.

The Houses on the Lake

Our street seems to be particularly active, with two houses besides my own that I know of having some type of paranormal activity. Although sporadic in nature, the phenomenon itself is still intriguing. What's so curious about it is that our houses are in very close proximity to each other; one is across the street from mine, and the other is two doors down from the house across the street. My husband and I are friends with both couples and I've been to their houses frequently.

The House Across the Street

A young couple lives in one of the houses, and the husband travels somewhat frequently for his job. It seems that every time he's gone, a young man, approximately sixteen years old, will appear at the end of the wife's bed.

He wears a black leather jacket and jeans. He doesn't really attempt to communicate with her; he will just stand there and look at her—quite unnerving to say the least. Then he will slowly fade away into nothingness once he's sure he's managed to wake her up and has her full attention.

If the young man doesn't appear, then an old African-American woman will appear. This woman is always in a rocking chair, slowing going back and forth, while staring at the young woman.

The curious thing is, the young couple doesn't have a rocking chair in their bedroom and have no idea who this woman is. This African-American woman seems to be a gentle soul, and will softly smile at the young woman before slowly disappearing.

I've been to their home on many occasions and have never sensed any type of spirit or other type of entity, but her husband has been home on most of my visits, and if he hasn't been home it was early in the evening when I was there. It seems, by her account, that these entities only visit late at night when her husband is out of town.

My belief is that the young man and the old woman in the rocking chair are there to bring her comfort and watch over her while her husband is out of town because there isn't any other paranormal activity in the home, and nothing happens when her husband is home. The ghosts aren't scaring my friend, simply startling her, which is a perfectly normal reaction.

As to where the ghosts are from, or how they got there, I have two possible theories.

My first theory is that they are two of the young woman's spirit guides or guardians, who appear to her in non-threatening ways in an attempt to make her feel safe while her husband is gone. This theory makes sense for the old woman in the rocking chair, because this spirit does acknowledge my friend by smiling at her. I'm not real sure this theory fits for the young man, who doesn't really make any attempt to communicate, but does make sure he's seen.

The second theory would be that they are displaced, and perhaps appear to my friend when her husband is out of town to let her know they are there. The young man in the leather jacket could have died in an accident on the old highway that was used before the current freeway was built; perhaps he is tied to the dirt from the road which was removed and used to build our subdivision. The older woman could have lived and died in a house that was destroyed when the freeway was constructed.

The fact that these spirits only appear when my friend's husband is out of town leads me to believe that the first theory is the correct line of thought in this mysterious, periodical haunting.

The House Two Doors Down

The house two doors down from this young couple is occupied by a totally different kind of ghost, who doesn't appear to shy away from making her presence known. She is also an intelligent spirit, which means that she goes out of her way to communicate with, and/or acknowledge the people living in the house.

It's believed that this phantom woman is the former owner of the house and just decided not to leave—and who can blame her? The house sits right on Lake St. Clair with a stupendous view and all the creature comforts—even if you're a ghost. The original house was built in the 1930s and was occupied by a woman and her husband. The husband passed away and then a few years later the woman died. Our friends bought the house some time ago and completely re-modeled the house, adding a second floor and expanding the original footprint of the house.

The first time the current owners saw their spectral houseguest was when she floated down the hallway, from the kitchen to the front door. The phantom had dark long hair and was dressed in a white nightgown; she paused long enough to acknowledge their presence before continuing upon her intended path. While this event did shake them up a bit, at that time they weren't big believers in the paranormal, but they are now.

The second time they saw her was when they were entertaining friends, and while they and their guests were talking in the large kitchen, the ghostly woman made an appearance in the middle of it all, before fading away. Needless to say, the homeowners were as shocked as the guests; all of them made an excuse to leave the party and made a rather hasty retreat.

One of the most interesting encounters with this phantom occurred when the couple was in bed sleeping. The man woke up and saw someone sitting on the foot of the bed. Thinking it was his wife, he sat up in bed and asked if everything was okay. That's when he realized his wife was still lying next to him, sound asleep!

He sat in shocked silence, watching the woman who sat quietly at the end of the bed until she turned around, smiled at him, and then got up and "walked" out of the bedroom and disappeared down the stairs. While he was tempted to follow their spectral guest, he thought it best to just stay put, although any further thoughts of sleep quickly vanished.

When this couple found out I was a paranormal investigator and a medium, they invited us over for dinner one night and brought up the topic of their ghost over appetizers.

Of course, no paranormal investigator worth their salt could pass up such an opportunity, so I began to roam around the house in search of their mystifying ghost. I found her in the den. I couldn't see her, but I could definitely pick up her energy.

"Hello," I greeted her.

It was then she allowed me to "see" her, yet she remained invisible to my friend.

"Who are you?" I asked telepathically.

"I used to live here. My husband and I built this home in 1936. I love it here so much," she explained.

"I understand," I told her.

"I try to stay out of the family's way, but sometimes I just get lonely and want them to know I'm still here. I mean them no harm and like them very much. I wish they'd talk to me more," she said wistfully.

"I'll see what I can do," I promised. "Have you crossed over, or do you need help?"

"No, I've crossed over. I just choose to come back from time to time. I enjoy the activity of the family and the children. Please don't make me leave," she pleaded.

"I won't. You're fine. I'll explain things to the family," I said.

"Thank you." She smiled at me and I felt her energy leave the space.

I explained to the family what the woman had told me, and they seemed relieved to find out it was the previous owner. They also said they had no problem with the woman coming back to visit from time to time. In fact, they seemed to enjoy the thought.

This type of spirit is not uncommon. When they die, many people choose to return to a place they loved when they were alive, even though they've crossed over.

My Shadow Man

When we purchased this house seven years ago, everything seemed fine at first. We were busy unpacking and getting everything settled. Quite honestly, I never really noticed anything "off" about the house and was perfectly content.

Then one night after we'd lived there less than six months, as I was watching television, I noticed two of my cats staring intently at the staircase that sits back and to the right of the couch. I turned to look at what they saw and noticed the shadow of a man walking slowly down the stairs. It was just an outline, but I could distinctly make out the shape of a rather large man, and I could see his shadowy, beefy fingers wrapped around the stair rail as he descended the staircase.

"What the hell?" I twisted my body to get a better look at the being.

As soon as I spoke, the shadow man darted down the stairs at lightning speed and disappeared. I leaped off the couch and moved quickly across the room to find out where the shadow man went, but there wasn't a trace of him to be found. I couldn't even feel any residual energy from my unexpected houseguest.

My thirty years as a paranormal investigator taught me that shadow people are benign creatures who make no attempt to communicate with the living. Many people feel that shadow people are a form of "watchers," who merely observe the living carry out their day-to-day activities.

However, there are also those who believe that shadow people are a form of demon, because there have been reports of shadow people with red eyes. I haven't personally encountered such a creature, but I have no doubt they exist due to the number of reports I've read.

I can only speak from my own personal experience with these entities, and have always found them to be shy creatures who will disappear as quickly as possible when they are spotted by the living.

My shadow person only appears from time to time and always in the same place, coming up or going down the stairs to the second floor of my home. Sometimes, he is quickly followed by a woman wearing a floor-length, white dress with a train. While I've only caught glimpses of the woman, I've seen the edge of her train cascade through the spindles of the staircase on several occasions.

Who she is and why she's here remains a mystery. I can't even say for sure whether or not she's attached in some way to the shadow man, but I highly doubt it. Shadow people don't make attachments, as far as I know, to other ghosts or spirits.

This woman isn't around long enough for me to even begin to make contact with her, nor does she make any attempt to interact with me, and I'm not even sure she's aware of my presence.

It could be that this mysterious woman is simply residual energy and not really a ghost at all.

Morrow Road

No book of ghost stories by a Michigan author is complete without the inclusion of the alleged Morrow Road haunting. The legend of Morrow Road is one of the most infamous tales in the world of ghost hunting, and takes place about an hour from where I live.

The story goes that a mother ran outside in the middle of the night to find her young son, who'd somehow gotten out of the house. How she and her son died is up for speculation, but the most popular theory is that because it was winter, the mother and son froze to death. The time period when this occurred is not recorded in history, and research has not divulged whether or not this event actually happened, or whether it's simply local legend.

The type of paranormal activity that allegedly occurs on Morrow Road varies. Many people claim that when you are on a certain bridge on the road, you will see a woman in a blood soaked nightgown carrying her dead child.

Others have claimed that an unexplainable green light charges them while on the road; still others claim to hear a baby crying at night, or have the feeling that someone is watching them from the woods. Still others have reported seeing ghostly, dark apparitions walking down the street, but they disappear once discovered.

When people found out I'm a paranormal investigator, they immediately asked me if I've been to Morrow Road, which is how I found out about this place to begin with. So, I began digging a little deeper and decided to talk to some of the older residents who'd been in this area their entire lives.

When you talk to some of the locals, they will tell you that the story was made up in the 1950s to keep teenagers from going to the desolate road. Now, I don't know about you, but if I were a teenager and I heard that story, it would be the first place I'd head.

I've investigated Morrow Road several times at different hours and during different seasons of the year, but not once have I had anything even remotely paranormal happen. This doesn't mean the legend isn't true, it just means nothing happened when I was there.

Investigation of county records during the time this incident allegedly took place did turn up several incidences of mothers and children dying in the area, however the locations of their deaths were unclear in the documents I've found. It's important to point out that typhoid fever, scarlet fever, and other diseases were running rampant through the area at the time, as well.

So the question really is: is Morrow Road haunted? That's an impossible question to answer. But, I believe the urban legend of Morrow Road will live on for many years to come.

First House on the Right

Out in the middle of nowhere, in southeastern Michigan, stands a deserted house that used to belong to a woman of considerable age. She didn't have much family, and the family she did have lived out of state.

I accidentally stumbled upon the property while driving down an unfamiliar road one fall afternoon, while out exploring the new area we'd just moved into. I still can't say for sure what made me look to my right as I passed the house, but when I saw it, I knew I had to turn around and explore this piece of property—there was just something about the energy emitting from the place that caught my attention.

I turned around on the dirt road, and pulled into the beaten-down tire path that served as a driveway. As I walked around the house, I felt that something didn't want me around there or inside the home, which, of course, made me even more curious. Not having enough time to explore further, I marked the house on my GPS and continued my trek into town to meet a friend for breakfast.

After ordering, I asked my friend about the house I'd spotted on the way. She said that Maggie Johnson, the woman who owned the home, died about a year ago. The family just abandoned the house and all of Maggie's personal belongings. Since her death, some of the townsfolk have reported some strange things going on at the property.

Some people have reported walking around the house, and when they looked into one of the living room windows, they noticed a white mist in the shape of a partial body. They could make out the arms and the outline of the head. They also reported that the white mist appeared to float across the living room before disappearing entirely.

I couldn't get the house out of my head all day, and I knew that any attempts at sleep would be futile until I satisfied my curiosity. That night, I slipped out of my mom's house and drove to Maggie Johnson's house.

Armed only with a flashlight, since I hadn't planned on ghost hunting while up north, I cautiously made my way through the tall grass and weeds that surrounded the house.

I paused by the large living room window, and as I went to peek inside, something pushed me hard away from the house, causing me to fall to the ground. I leaped to my feet and shined my flashlight in all directions, but no one or nothing was in sight. In addition, if someone had been there, I would have heard them walking through the tall grass and dead, crunchy leaves that littered the area from the tall trees surrounding the property.

As much as I wanted to investigate this event further, I didn't want to trespass into the house, and I was completely alone in the middle of the night on an all-but-deserted street, where the houses are miles apart. Furthermore, whatever pushed me obviously didn't want me there, and I interpreted the mild attack as a warning that I should leave.

I made my way to my car and looked back at the house. In the upstairs window, I saw an eerie light that appeared to move around the room. I knew there was no one in the house and had no explanation for the light. The area around the house is quite deserted for miles and there are no streetlights. The night I was there was a cloudy night, with no moon.

On several occasions while at the property, I've felt ice-cold breezes push against me when I was right next to the house. It appears that Maggie Johnson is still living in the house, long after her death, and doesn't want anyone to disturb her or her property.

Several times since that night I've visited the home, but, not wanting to upset whatever spirit is there, I haven't made any attempt to enter the space.

The house has fallen into a horrible state of disrepair and someone has boarded up the windows on the first floor, which has done little to deter intruders who have decimated the place.

The Jenkins House

On the outskirts of a small harbor town, nestled on the shores of Lake St. Clair in southeastern Michigan, sits a pre–Civil War, two-story farmhouse. There's nothing really unusual about the appearance of the white clapboard house from the outside … unless you count the old woman sitting in the front window. Funny thing about that woman—she died more than fifty years ago.

The many owners of the property, most of whom are descendants of Matthew Jenkins, the original owner of the home, have observed many paranormal events.

One woman remembers living in the house as a child, when one night she and her sister went downstairs to get a drink of water. As they passed by one of the parlors, they saw a soft light emanating from the room.

When they peered into the parlor, they were shocked to see a large table sitting in the middle of the room, which shouldn't have been there, as they didn't even own a table like that. What was even more astonishing is that a dead body was lying on the table. The room was filled with a lot of people dressed in black clothing, in a fashion that was common during the Victorian era.

Rooted to the floor by fear, they stood transfixed by the scene before them. Then they noticed that all the activity in the room had ceased, and the phantom apparitions were staring at them! Not wanting to see what was going to happen next, they raced up to their bedrooms. The next morning, everything was back to normal in the "funeral" parlor.

The same girls also reported seeing a gorgeous young blond woman standing in their bedroom one night. The ghost was holding a candle and motioned for the girls to follow her, but they were too scared to do so. They turned on a light and the vision disappeared.

Unable to resist such tempting tales of paranormal activity, a friend of mine we'll call Monica and I decided to conduct our own investigation into the paranormal activity at this house.

After getting permission from the current owner, a man from out of town, to enter the property, we spent considerable time exploring the house's many rooms. At this time the house was vacant, because the current owner was in the process of renovating it. Over time, the house had fallen into a state of great disrepair.

As we walked through the house, we couldn't help but feel we were being watched by someone or something unseen. When we were on the second-floor hallway, I heard Monica scream! When I turned around, Monica was gone and there was a gaping hole in the floor!

"Monica, where are you? Are you okay?" I yelled frantically.

"I'm down here. I'm fine!" she said.

"Where's here?" I asked.

"I don't know!" Monica replied.

"Hang tight. I'll find you." I scrambled down the stairs and looked around the house, but I couldn't find Monica.

"Bang on a wall," I yelled.

Monica start banging and I traced the noise to the large closet under the stairs that led to the second floor. I flung open the door; the closet was empty, but I could hear Monica close by.

I started banging on the walls of the closet, and the side wall, which I quickly discovered was a hidden panel door.

Finally it yielded and swung open—it was on hinges! Monica came scrambling up two stairs to freedom.

We then returned to the small room she'd fallen into, a room of approximately ten feet by fifteen feet. The walls were constructed of fieldstone, and were held in place by mortar or some other type of material. On the sand floor sat benches that went around almost the entire room. We'd heard that the Jenkins house might have been on the Underground Railroad, and now we were pretty sure we had proof. We asked the remaining family members about the hidden room, but they denied any knowledge of it.

We spent a couple of days doing research on the house and came to the conclusion that the woman many people reported seeing in the front window was the mother of one of the former owners. Apparently, she died in the exact room the apparition appears and was known, when alive, to sit in front of the window for hours.

On another occasion, Monica and a friend of hers went back to the house to conduct some more research. They were on the second floor and when they walked by one of the bedroom windows they saw a large, glowing white figure run across the front yard of the house. At that very same moment, they heard a man's voice yell, "Get out! Get out!" from the same room they were in. It sounded as if the man was standing right next to them! Not wasting a moment, they fled from the house.

Monica and her friend went back to the house a couple days later and found an old book in one of the upstairs bedrooms. The book contained the genealogy of the Jenkins family.

Wanting to make copies of the book, Monica, without asking permission, took it home with her and spent almost the entire night reading the book. The next day, Monica and her friend drove by the house and stopped in front of it. She saw a large man with a full beard and mustache staring down at her. Monica knew it was Matthew Jenkins, due to the pictures we'd found while conducting our research into the history of the house.

From the moment they saw the man, they both became very ill. They experienced unexplained nausea and vomiting. It went on for a couple of days. During that period, I talked to Monica and she finally told me about the book they'd found, the man they saw at the Jenkins house, and how sick she was.

"It's the book," I told her. "You've got to put back the book. I'll meet you at the house."

A few minutes later, I pulled into the driveway of the house and found Monica waiting for me with the large book in her arms. Monica looked pale and weak.

We both gazed up at the house and in the far left, second-story bedroom window, I saw the apparition of the man Monica told me about.

"He wants the book back," I told Monica. "You stole part of his family."

"I didn't steal anything," Monica said. "I borrowed the book."

"Without permission," I explained. "Come on. Let's go."

"I'm not going in there with that man in there." Monica shook her head.

"Give me the damn book," I sighed. "I'll do it. Where did you find this book?"

"In the room the man was in. It was on the stop shelf of the closet," Monica said.

"Fine! But don't ever take anything from any house again. Got it?"

"Got it," Monica said, handing me the book and the key to the house, which the current owner had given us.

I let myself in the back door and made my way through the large kitchen area to the staircase at the front of the house. I tentatively climbed the stairs to the second floor.

"Mr. Jenkins, I know you're upset about the book being taken, but I'm here to bring it back. My friend didn't know what she was doing, and I'm very sorry. Nothing like this will ever happen again," I explained to the spirit as I walked toward the bedroom.

I peered into the bedroom, but didn't see or feel the spirit. I walked across the room to the big closet and put the large book on the top shelf. I pushed it as far back as it would go—virtually hiding it from sight. When I turned around to leave the bedroom, I felt the spirit standing in front of the window on the opposite side of the room.

"Goodbye, Mr. Jenkins. I hope you find peace," I said, as I walked out of the bedroom toward the staircase. I let myself out the back door and rejoined Monica by the cars.

"I'm keeping the key to the house," I told her. "I'll get it back to the owner of the property."

"But what if I want to go back in the house?" Monica said.

"You're not going back into the house. Your exploring-haunted-houses days are over, unless you're with me. You just can't seem to stay out of trouble," I teased her.

"True." She gave me a wry smile.

We both got into our cars, took one more look at the house, and drove away.

That was the last time I was in the house. The owners of the property spent several months lovingly restoring it to its former glory. They report that the paranormal activity has all but subsided, with the exception of one thing.

They always find the window open in the first floor bedroom—the very same room where the woman died—where she sits and stares forlornly out the window, into the front yard of the farmhouse.

While the current owners are aware of the history of the house, to them the rich history of the property makes the house more desirable. Monica spoke to the new owners after contacting one of the surviving relatives of the original owner, and verified as much information as she could.

Chapter 8

THE HOUSE OF HORRORS

To the casual observer, the old abandoned farmhouse that sits in the middle of nowhere, in upstate Iowa, wouldn't even register in their minds as being a place of interest.

However, to those who have lived in that farmhouse, or crossed the threshold at one time or another, it is a house of terror-filled nights and tense, uneasy days. You see, the land and the house that no one really pays any attention to, are among the most haunted places I've personally ever heard of.

In all fairness, the house itself is not to blame. Before this house was built, another stood in its place. However, when the original house was torn down, the basement wasn't removed, and the current home stands on the original foundation.

The catalyst that set off the tragic chain of events throughout the years all began with the land itself. Long ago, there was a Native American encampment in the woods behind where the house now stands. While history doesn't tell us what exactly happened, it does tell us that the Native Americans were massacred.

The event was so traumatic that there have been reports of people seeing the ghosts of Native Americans still crossing the property. It's my belief that this catastrophic event caused the land itself to become stained or cursed.

When this happens, any building or other structures and the people who inhabit them will also become victims of the massacre that took place so many years ago.

The land itself now holds the house, three silos, an old barn that pre-dates the house, a garage, and a long-abandoned chicken coop. There have been reports of paranormal activity occurring everywhere on the property, with the exception of the chicken coop and silos, as far as I know.

The long list of horrors that occurred after the massacre started when an influenza outbreak raced through the area in the mid- to late-1800s. At that time, there was a family with eight children living in the original home. Seven of the children died during the plague.

That house was eventually torn down and the existing house was built on the old foundation. According to lore, two little boys drowned in the ditch that lies at the front of the property during a flash flood. To this day, the spirits of the two boys can often be seen in the ditch, reliving the tragedy that befell them all those years ago. No one is quite sure when this happened, but it's believed to be sometime in the 1940s.

Adding to the list of horrors that occurred on the land is the story of a carpetbagger who was staying in the barn for a night. He was found murdered the next morning. History doesn't tell us who the man was, or whether his murder was ever solved, but according to the local historian, the event did take place, although he wouldn't reveal his sources.

History does tell us that a man committed suicide in the home, although the details are sketchy at best. His ghost has been seen in the upstairs bedroom closet, so it's assumed he hanged himself in that closet. This apparition has been seen many times throughout the years, by the various owners of the property.

One of the families that lived in the house employed a housekeeper who disappeared under what is termed "mysterious circumstances," but no details were included in the paper. In fact, no one's exactly sure if she disappeared by her own accord or if she was murdered. What is known is that the ghost of a woman who's believed to be the housekeeper, according to people who knew her when she was alive, appears on the staircase in the home from time to time.

Other ghostly activity around the property includes reports of disembodied voices and shadows. There have also been reports of a man hanging in the barn and two other men hanging in the garage—although no one knows who the men are or why they were hanged.

One of the sadder stories surrounding the house is that of a little girl who lived there at one time, who fell down the stairs. She broke her neck and died. What is presumed to be her ghost can still be seen skipping through the house, although she seems to prefer to hang out around the back porch of the house.

Perhaps the most intriguing story of all about this property happened in the recent past. A man and his wife bought the property sometime in the late 1960s or early 1970s.

They lived there in what seemed to be perfect harmony, until one day the husband disappeared. The wife told everyone who asked that her husband abandoned her, and she soon moved out of the house but continues to own the property. However, given some bone-chilling events that have occurred in the house since, her story becomes rather suspect.

Since the husband's disappearance, the wife has rented out the house to various people who, by all accounts, didn't remain there very long. The house was rented out to a young family, who, by the way, are the last people to ever live in this house. They were thrilled to have such a large house. Regrettably, their euphoria didn't last long.

Not long after moving in, the family began to experience eerie paranormal activity.

Their son, as did other members of the family, reported seeing a man in the closet of one of the bedrooms. It's assumed this is the phantom of the man who hanged himself. On several occasions, the young housewife would be pushed toward the closet where the man committed suicide.

As if that wasn't enough, the family would wake up every morning to find furniture and other objects moved around the house. In some cases, items would disappear altogether, especially objects kept in the kitchen. The television, washer, dryer, and microwave would also turn on by themselves.

The family began searching for a logical explanation for the strange events, so they called out an electrician to check the wiring, but no problems could be found with the wiring or the appliances.

It didn't take long for the family to become terrified of their house, but with little money and an ironclad lease, they felt they had no choice but to stay. I suspect the lease was intentionally made so binding because of the mass exodus of previous tenants.

One of the most terrifying events in the house occurred when the young mother was walking by the basement door and something unseen gave her a hard shove toward the basement stairs. Luckily, she was able to catch herself before tumbling down the staircase to the hard floor of the basement.

Naturally, her husband became quite concerned about the unseen and seemingly negative ghosts in the house that were terrorizing and physically attacking his family, so he decided to investigate.

He made his way down to the basement and discovered an old cistern that had been sealed up. Judging by the appearance of the concrete, it hadn't been sealed that long ago.

Further exploration led him to a newly cinder-blocked section of the basement which was the size of a door. Given the close proximity to the furnace, the man assumed the room behind the cinder blocks was probably the old coal room, used when the house had a coal furnace.

As he was making his way back to the staircase leading up to the kitchen, paint cans that had been stored on a shelf began to propel themselves off the shelf and pelted the man harshly.

Screaming in pain and fear, he covered his head with his arms and quickly made his way across the basement to the staircase. He rushed up the stairs, slammed the basement door behind him, and slid the lock into place—an act of futility because the next morning, the basement door was standing wide open.

That was the last straw. The family quickly packed up their belongings, threw them into the back of the husband's pickup truck, and fled the property in fear.

That should be the end of this story, right? Unfortunately it's not.

You see, the young housewife had an affinity for mirrors and enjoyed etching mirrors. When they moved into the house, a large mirror was on the mantle of the fireplace in the living room. The day they fled the house in panic, the woman grabbed the mirror off of the mantel and took it with them to their new home.

Much to their horror, soon after moving into their new house, the same type of activity they'd fled began to happen again. Furniture and other objects would be moved, unexplained voices could be heard, the appliances would turn themselves on, etc. This is when I was called in by a friend of the family's, to figure out what was going on.

After hearing the whole story, one thing became perfectly clear: one of the most menacing entities that resided in their old house had come with them to their new home, and it was more than likely attached to the mirror.

The reason for this is that mirrors can act as a portal between the world of the living and the world of the dead. Ghosts, spirits, and any other types of entity can freely pass through this portal, as easily as you or I can walk through an open door.

In addition, it's not uncommon for a spirit to attach itself to an object made of any porous material such as stone or wood. Thus, if the object is moved from place to place, or house to house, the spirit attached to that object would move right along with it.

To make matters worse, the young woman was emotionally unstable, and any etching she did on the mirror would only serve to invite a negative entity through the mirror and into their home.

Certain types of entities feed on negative emotions, or emotional upheaval, which feeds the entities and can make them stronger and more powerful than they already are.

My advice to the family was to immediately get rid of the mirror they'd brought with them from the other house. The wife was reluctant to do so, but the husband grabbed the mirror, took it outside, and shattered it into a million pieces in the garbage can. He then removed the garbage can from the property and drove it out to a local landfill where it remains to this day. Since the husband got rid of the mirror, the family is not experiencing any further paranormal activity.

My friend, whom I'll call Kelly, lives near this house of horrors; she found the reported paranormal activity at the house irresistible, and is the person who initially told me about this house. So of course, she had to go check it out for herself.

She was curious as to whether the removal, and eventual destruction, of the mirror that once resided over the mantel had caused any paranormal activity to stop completely. Since the house was not lived in, and completely void of any furnishings (not to mention the home had been condemned), she made a beeline for the property.

Upon arriving at the house, she first inspected the garage. As she explored the space, she heard a noise behind her and turned around to see the shadows of two men hanging from the rafters of the garage, slowly swinging back and forth like pendulums on an old grandfather clock. Frozen in place, she stared in wonder at the two apparitions for a few seconds before snapping herself out of her trancelike state, and quickly exited the garage. Kelly isn't sure how long the apparitions hung around, pardon the pun, but she didn't stick around the garage long enough to find out.

Undaunted, she walked across the yard to the farmhouse. Upon entering the house, Kelly walked around the living room, not really noticing anything out of the ordinary.

She wandered around the second floor of the old house, tentatively checking every floorboard for sturdiness before taking each step, as the house was condemned and not in very good repair. Again, everything seemed to be in order, so she headed back down the staircase and into the kitchen.

As Kelly roamed around the kitchen, the air became heavy and she was finding it hard to breathe. It felt as though all the air in the room was being sucked out by a vacuum.

Deciding to leave, she headed for the door to the back yard that lay on the opposite side of the kitchen. As she passed by the basement door, an unseen arm grabbed her around the waist and tried to drag her into the basement!

Kelly struggled to get free as this unseen entity inched her closer and closer to the basement stairs. Kelly was terrified and wrestled frantically to get away. She realized it pointless was to try to grab an arm she couldn't even see.

"Let go of me!" she screamed, and with one final burst of energy she broke free from the entity and raced out the door in a blind panic. She leaped into her car and raced out of the driveway, only stopping when she felt she was far enough away to be out of the reach of the house and the entities that resided there.

After Kelly caught her breath, she called me and relayed the details of what just happened to her.

While I sympathized with her experience, I also admonished her for going out to that place by herself, knowing what type of seemingly dangerous paranormal activity occurred there. Kelly hasn't been back to the property since her terrifying encounter with the unknown entity.

While it appears that this house and property have an overabundance of paranormal activity, in reality there's only one intelligent entity that occupies the home—the entity that tried to pull Kelly into the basement.

The two little boys by the ditch, the little girl that runs through the house, the men hanging in the garage and barn, and the eerie sight of the ghosts of the Native Americans roaming around the property, would be considered a residual haunting, in my opinion. Residual hauntings aren't ghosts; they represent the energy of past events, replayed over and over again.

It's the entity in the basement that personally has me intrigued. While it may appear to be a violent, malevolent spirit, I'm not convinced it is. I believe the spirit is desperate.

Given that facts of the land and house as we know them, it would make sense that either the housekeeper's or missing husband's body is hidden somewhere in the basement, and is frantically trying to get someone's attention.

As I understand it, the only two places a body could be hidden in the basement of the house are in the sealed cistern or in the sealed old coal room. If you really examine this case, it's about the only thing that makes sense.

The spirit has, at least twice that we are aware of, tried to get someone into the basement. Once, when it pushed Kelly's friend toward the basement stairs and again, when it tried to pull Kelly toward the basement.

A desperate spirit will exhibit seemingly violent behavior, when in reality the poor spirit is only trying to get someone's attention.

The paranormal team I belong to, Black River Paranormal, intends to visit this site in the summer of 2014, and try to determine what exactly is going on there and, perhaps, rescue a spirit that is in desperate need. We know very few people know about the house, well … up until now, but we also know that because we've protected the property by not giving out the location, it will be there waiting for us when we arrive. We also know that there aren't any paranormal teams in the area or who know the location of the property, so it will be a virgin ghost hunt—meaning it's never before been investigated by a ghost hunting team. Ahhhh, paradise!

Chapter 9

The Haunted Land

Our paranormal investigation team, Black River Paranormal, was called out to a house by a woman and her husband. They'd been experiencing a plethora of paranormal activity that included being pushed, shoved, and scratched while in the house.

We arrived at the modular house early in the evening and, when we entered the property, discovered that the woman's sister and her three adult children were also present. While none of these other people lived in the home, it was good to have them there, as they had all experienced some type of paranormal activity in the house.

While the team began setting up the equipment and two other members were talking to the homeowners, I walked through the house to get a feel for the energy and to see if I could locate the spirit they were complaining about.

As I walked through the house, I couldn't help but notice all the religious symbols displayed throughout the home. There were numerous crosses on the walls, a large open Bible on the coffee table, along with a Bible in every room, including the bathrooms, and bowls of sea salt in every room. These people were terrified—that much was obvious.

Because the house was small, it wasn't hard to hear the conversation going on in the dining room. The homeowners, whom we'll call Shelly and Rodger, were experiencing a surplus of paranormal events.

Rodger reported being pushed several times while he was in the bathroom, and Shelly felt like she was constantly being watched by a malevolent entity. In addition, items were being moved or sometimes thrown across a room, some of the crosses would fall off the wall without explanation, and the Bible on the coffee table would be violently slammed shut by something unseen.

Shelly and Rodger were convinced they had a demon, but I wasn't so sure. The energy I felt in the house did not contain the energy of a demonic entity, but rather a ghost of someone who, when alive, walked this Earth in human form. The energy of this ghost, however, did feel very angry and menacing, but not diabolical.

Shelly and Rodger also reported seeing the ghosts of a man and a woman, dressed in clothing from the 1800s, who they felt were trying to make contact with them. The phantom couple would beckon them, but neither Rodger nor Shelly ever got up the nerve to heed the request—understandably so. They also reported that the paranormal activity began right after their landlord, who was a rather mean man, died two years ago. Before that, they'd lived in the house for five years without incident.

One of the sons then brought out a large cardboard box from the top shelf of the front closet. He opened the box to reveal several plastic bags, partially filled with Native American arrowheads, which the family found on and near the property.

What really shocked me was that each bag contained a picture of one of the members of the family. Shelly told me they did this to show who found what so that each family member would know which arrowheads were theirs.

What they didn't realize was that by putting a picture of a family member in each bag, the potential was there to draw the spirits of the Native Americans that once made and owned the arrowheads to them, thereby making them targets—should the spirits of the Native Americans choose to make themselves known.

We already knew from our research that Native Americans were in the area many years ago, however we weren't able to discern if there'd been some type of attack or massacre of the Native Americans on or near the property.

It's never a good idea to keep any type of picture of yourself or a member of your family in a bag with any type of relics, no matter where the relics came from. There's a theory among some paranormal researchers that says it could be possible, although very rare, that the spirits of the people who once crafted the relics could be drawn to the energy of the person whose picture is in a bag with the relics. This is not just a Native American thing, but applies to anything and anybody, no matter their ethnic background.

We also knew that a fire raced through the area in the early 1800s, and that not only was there a foundation of an old house next door, but also another on the edge of the woods that bordered their property. We didn't research the property next door, because that was not the focus of our investigation. The home Roger and Shelly lived in didn't appear on the scene until the mid-1990s, long after the great fire of the 1800s.

It quickly became evident that we were dealing with more than one entity, and all of these spectral beings were tied to the property in one way or another! It also became readily apparent that we were dealing with a much more complicated case than we originally thought.

After a brief team meeting, outside the earshot of the homeowners and their family, we came up with a plan of action: I'd walk the property, the house, and the remains of the burned-out house next door and see what I picked up. Then we'd decide on the proper course of action for each place, gather the necessary equipment, and return the following weekend to execute the plan.

I walked out the back door of the house and made my way through the massive backyard to the small grove of woods at the back of the property. I allowed the energy, which was almost palpably radiating from the woods, to wash over me, and I could "see" a group of Native American men and one chief or shaman—I couldn't be sure which, standing in a row just inside the tree line.

Because I wasn't sure if I was a welcomed visitor, I stopped a respectful distance away from the spirits and waited to see if they would acknowledge me. I could now make out more details of the phantom beings, and was almost positive the leader was a shaman, based upon the long staff in his hand and the few feathers that adorned his long hair. I'd run across many Native American spirits before and have always found them to be rather open and friendly.

The shaman held up his hand and motioned me to follow him deeper into the woods. Still keeping a respectful distance, I obliged and as quietly as possible followed the ghost along an old trail, noticing that the group of four or five other Native American men fell in line behind me.

I have to admit this made me rather uncomfortable, since I didn't understand their intention as of yet, but their energy didn't feel malevolent so I made no attempt to head for the safety of the house.

We walked in silence a short way through the woods before the shaman stopped and pointed to a rather deep hole in the ground. Getting the distinct impression the shaman wanted me to look in the approximately one-foot-deep and four-foot-wide hole, I carefully scrambled down the slight embankment and began to clear away sticks, leaves, and other debris that'd accumulated throughout the years.

Underneath all the ground cover, I found a long staff made out of an old tree branch. The top of the staff appeared to have been carved hollow when it was made, and it appeared as though some type of square-bottomed object was once attached to the staff.

With the staff in my hand, I looked up from the hole I was standing in to look at the Native American ghosts that surrounded me. The shaman bowed slightly and all the ghosts simply vanished. I spent a little more time exploring the location where I found the staff, but I found nothing else of any relevance.

As I walked back to the house, I made a mental note to make an offering the following weekend to the gentle Native American spirits.

To this day, I'm still not sure of the significance of the staff, but I choose to look upon it as a gift from the ghosts of the Native Americans that once so proudly roamed that land. It may be that the shaman gave me the staff as a sign of respect because, like the shaman once did, I deal with the spirit world. I still have the staff and it is proudly displayed in my office, as a reminder of that day.

Still pondering the event that just occurred, I turned my attention to the remains of the 1800s house that occupied the lot next to our clients' property. Accompanied by Randy, the founder of Black River Paranormal, and his trusty video camera, we made our way through the tall brush to the lot next door.

All that was left of the structure was the foundation and a few charred pieces of wood that were clinging to the home's remains, like a frightened child to its mother.

Randy turned on the video camera and began filming the session.

Within a few seconds of putting my hand on the burned wood, visions began to fill my head. They came so fast and furious, I had to make a conscious effort to slow them down so I could see what they were.

"This used to be a small cabin—two, maybe three, small rooms. I can't see it clearly because the only visible light is from the rush of flames streaking across the open field next to the house," I began.

In my vision, the fire was devouring everything in its path with a fury that only a raging fire can produce.

"The cabin was filled up with smoke and I can see a family lying in their beds, sleeping. They are completely unaware of the impending danger just outside their door.

"The man woke up and started coughing and gagging. I can see him leap out of bed and yell to his wife to get the children and her mother and get out of the house."

I saw the man run out the only door and his eyes grow wide at the sight of the angry flames, only a few short feet from their home.

"The man saw the fire and ran back inside. I can see him shaking his wife awake and helping her gather the two kids. The kids aren't moving and they aren't waking up," I said. "The smoke is so thick, the family seems to be disorientated and can't find the door to the house.

"I see them coughing and gagging. They got down on the floor and crawled across the floor inch by inch toward the door. The wife and her two children made it out the door before collapsing a few feet away from the home— over that way," I pointed.

"The man went back into the house to pull his mother-in-law to safety. He grabbed her and pushed her out the door. She stumbled a few feet and fell to the ground, next to her daughter and grandchildren.

"The man never made it back out of the house, and the woman, her children, and her mother lapsed into unconsciousness ten feet from the house and were ravaged by the fire."

I pulled my hand off the board and Randy and I stood in silence for a few moments as we imagined the terror that family must have experienced.

"Do you think this is the family our clients have seen?" Randy asked as he shut off the video camera.

"I'm not sure," I shrugged. "Let's see if we can make contact."

"Do what you do," Randy chuckled. He checked to make sure the video camera disc had enough time left before clicking it back on. "I'm just going to stand here and film."

Once again, I laid my hand upon the charred piece of wood and this time focused on one of the previous occupants of the house. Within a few moments, the spirit of the young wife and mother acknowledged telepathically that she was here.

"I've got the woman," I told Randy.

"Excellent. Ask her if it's her family that appears to our clients," Randy said.

"She says that it is them. Her family is trying to protect our clients from the other entity in the house. The male spirit that's in our client's house is not demonic, just not a nice man." I told Randy. "This woman's family desperately wants to cross over, but they are afraid. They don't want to leave one another in case one or more of them don't make it across to the other side, and they don't want to leave the family next door unprotected."

"Can you help them?" Randy asked.

"Yes. Definitely."

Telepathically, I told the woman spirit to have her family hold each other's hands and go into the light together, and that we would take care of the male spirit at the house next door.

In my mind's eye, I saw the family hold hands and walk into the light together, and once they did that, the energy of the burned-out cabin became lighter and more in line with the energy around it.

"They've crossed," I told Randy. "Let's head back to our client's house and try to figure out who's still there."

Randy turned off the video recorder and we slowly walked back to meet the rest of the team. I armed myself with a tape recorder and digital camera, while Randy changed the disc in the video camera. The rest of the team spread out through the house and began to investigate. Randy and I decided to investigate the bathroom, where much of the paranormal activity had occurred, and the bedrooms.

We spent the next two hours trying just about everything we could to get a response or to make contact with the malevolent entity in the house, but everything seemed quiet. I could feel the spirit's energy, but couldn't pinpoint where it was coming from. However, it felt strongest in the hallway leading from the living room down to the bedrooms.

"It's got to be around here somewhere," I told Randy.

Randy looked around the hallway, and then pointed up to the ceiling; there was a hatch leading to the attic.

"Good job! That's exactly where I think it is," I said. "I've got to get up in the attic."

It's not unusual for ghosts, spirits, or other types of entities to hide from paranormal investigators to avoid discovery, so we took this turn of events in stride.

Randy went into the kitchen and told the clients that we needed access to the attic area. One of the sons came out of the kitchen with a ladder and electric screwdriver, and unsealed the entrance to the attic. He then unfolded the set of stairs leading to the attic.

After handing the digital camera and tape recorder to Randy, I scrambled up the ladder to the entrance of the attic. Randy then handed me the camera and recording device.

"I know you're here," I announced. "Make your presence known."

Total silence, but I could feel the spirit's energy. I started to snap a few pictures.

"You can't hide from me," I told the spirit. "What do you want me to do?"

Again, my question was met with silence.

I grabbed the tape recorder and handed it down to Randy, along with my camera.

When I got out of the attic, Randy and I played back the tape. We were thrilled to realize we'd captured some EVPs, or electronic voice phenomena.

When I told the spirit I knew it was there, the response from the entity was, "Phillip is here." After I'd asked what the spirit wanted me to do we heard the word, "die."

We asked the clients if they knew anyone named Phillip who'd died, and they said that it was the name of their ex-landlord, who'd died two years ago. He'd been a really nasty person in life, and tormented his tenants in various ways. Apparently he was continuing the harassment after death, as well.

That's how it works, though: a person's personality doesn't really change after death, most times. It they're a mean person in life, generally they're going to be a nasty spirit in death. Likewise, if a person was nice in life, so they will be in death.

We told the clients we'd be back the next Saturday, packed up all the gear, and left.

The following weekend Randy and I returned with a baggie filled with loose tobacco and Indian corn kernels, a bottle of holy water, a smudge stick, and an extremely powerful spiritual warfare prayer which hopefully would drive Phillip from our clients' home.

The first thing we did was walk out to the edge of the woods at the back of the lot with the baggie, to make an offering to the Native American spirits that roamed the land. I've found that loose tobacco and corn kernels are two of the most respectful and prized gifts to Native American spirits.

While Randy filmed, I took a handful of the tobacco and corn mixture, and as I scattered it along the ground I said, "This offering is made to the spirits of the north and their wise grandfathers. It is my wish that you accept this gift as a token of respect and friendship." I repeated this process for each of the other three directions.

Now it was time to deal with Phillip. It's been my experience that, when dealing with the paranormal, it generally boils down to the age-old battle of light versus dark, good versus evil. Sometimes you win, sometimes you lose, and sometimes you have to settle for an uneasy balance between the two. The battle with Phillip was one I planned on being able to chalk up in the win column.

I knew from previous experiences with malevolent spirits that they wouldn't leave by their own accord—they had to be forced out. While there are many ways to do this, I use holy water, a powerful prayer that banishes negative spirits and/or energy, and then finish with a good smudging of the location. I prefer to use smudge sticks that are a combination of white sage and sweet grass. The white sage dispels negative energy, while the sweet grass fills a space with positive energy.

Before starting, I made sure all the windows and doors were tightly shut, with the exception of the farthest east exit of the house, which in this case turned out to be a sliding glass door. I do this because I want the spirit to have only one way out.

Starting at the far west corner of the house, I began by wetting my finger with holy water and making the sign of the cross on every window, door, and jamb, as I recited the spiritual warfare prayer.

I kept repeating this procedure throughout the house, making my way from room to room. I also went back up in the attic and performed this ritual here, as well. I didn't want to give Phillip any place to hide. I finished up at the sliding glass door in the kitchen. I then repeated this process, fanning the smoke from the smudge stick into every nook and cranny with a feather, and reciting the same prayer I'd used with the holy water. Once both rituals were complete, I shut the sliding glass door, marked it with the sign of the cross, and smudged it completely.

During these rituals, an old clock the homeowners had hanging on the wall in the living room struck twelve. Randy and I both found this fascinating, because the actual time was 1:15 p.m. and the clock that chimed twelve was reading 1:15, not twelve o'clock.

Also during this process, Randy got a text on his cell phone that read, "Leaving now, but don't want to go." The text was from one of his friends, but when he called her back after we were finished, she said she was out of town with friends, and hadn't texted him in over a week. Randy had her check her cell phone, and it showed no record of any text being sent to Randy that day. His friend was just as mystified by this event as Randy and I were.

Once Phillip left, you could feel the energy of the whole house change. It became lighter and fresher. I walked through the house one more time just to make sure, and then, knowing my work was done, we left.

Last time Randy checked with the client, an electrical fire had burned down the house—how ironic. But before that, they hadn't experienced any additional paranormal activity. They were planning to rebuild on the property.

Chapter 10

THE CEMETERY OF RESTLESS SOULS

Contrary to what many people believe, it's actually very rare for a cemetery to be haunted. This is because after they die, many people come back in phantom form, to visit people they loved when they were alive or a place that holds fond memories. Since most living people have no emotional tie to a cemetery, there is no reason to haunt it when they die. But, as with everything else, there are exceptions. The following stories are just two examples of cemeteries that are haunted.

As I drove through the front gates of the cemetery I was visiting, I became excited to see where my ancestors were buried and the secrets to my family's past I may discover. My first thought was that Alfred Hitchcock would have loved this place so much, he would have filmed a movie here.

Allowing my eyes to take in the landscape, I couldn't help but notice that this graveyard hungrily devours acres of land, creeps over tiered hills, and shrouds itself among a forest of tall shade trees. Regal but small mausoleums with elaborate stained-glass windows dot the landscape and stand as grim reminders of a more elegant and sophisticated era.

An eerie fog rolled in off the neighboring lake, illuminated by the sun rays filtering through tentacle-like tree branches, as it slipped its way through the cemetery, giving it a foreboding and mysterious appearance.

After stopping at the office to get a map and the location of my ancestors' graves, I slowly maneuvered my Jeep along the twisting roads toward the back of the cemetery. A carpet of colorful fall leaves guided me as I drove by various sections, such as the Garden of Serenity and the Sanctuary of Eternal Peace, finally bringing the car to a stop in front of the Gates of Salvation, the section my relatives are buried in—which would make perfect sense if you knew my family.

I was delighted to discover that three generations of my ancestors occupy a large family plot, and I began taking pictures and making notes of names, dates, and any other information I could obtain by reading the headstones.

Even though the cemetery office was making copies for me, of all the information they have on my relatives, I wanted to take my own notes as well, for comparison.

While cemeteries normally don't creep me out, I couldn't shake the feeling that I was being watched closely by someone or something. I kept looking around to see if there was anyone else close by, but I saw no one.

Not being able to concentrate on the task at hand, I decided to explore a little bit more of the cemetery. I meandered over to one of the mausoleums and peeked through the stained-glass window; weird I know, but such things are sometimes irresistible. I saw a small altar at the back of the mausoleum and six caskets, three on each side, neatly stacked on shelves, as if the bodies had been filed away in a cabinet for future reference.

About ten yards away, I spotted a large statue of a winged angel and began to wander in that direction; the leaves crunched under my feet as I walked past a high row of hedges that separated one section of the cemetery from another.

It was then I realized that mine were not the only footsteps in the dry leaves; there was someone walking behind the hedges. To make sure, I stopped walking and heard the distinct sound of two footsteps in the leaves, but whoever it was remained hidden behind the bushes.

Cautiously, I made my way to the end of the run of hedges and peered around the corner. No one was in sight and the footsteps stopped. I quickly ran out to an open area to look around, but there wasn't anyone there, and I didn't see the cars of any other mourners parked in the vicinity.

I put out my psychic feelers and picked up on the residual energy of a spirit, but I couldn't detect any type of ghost around me. Whatever ghost walked along with me was long gone.

Frustrated, I continued to explore, and stopped only to read inscriptions on old tombstones, and to admire the period architecture of some of the mausoleums. It wasn't long before I felt spirits gathering around me in the cemetery, yet they stayed a respectful distance away until I returned to the grave plot of my ancestors. I kept trying to communicate with them, but they wouldn't engage in conversation.

The longer I stayed in the cemetery, the more unnerved I became, and soon it became almost impossible to concentrate on my task. It felt as if a lot of people were closing in on me and I began to feel claustrophobic, even though I was in a relatively open area.

I sat down on the ground and closed my eyes. Taking a deep breath, I allowed my energy to open up and spread out away from me in all directions, in an attempt to figure out who or what was around me.

Much like a radio frequency, I adjusted my energy lower and lower, until I picked up three distinct spirits around me. Opening my eyes, I slowly scanned the area and saw a dark shadow in the rough shape of a person dart from behind a tree and disappear behind one of the mausoleums.

I stood up and began to walk toward the mausoleum. Within a few minutes, I realized that I was almost completely surrounded by dark shadows, and the rest of the ghosts scattered when these shadows showed up. Although the shadows stayed far enough away that I could barely detect them, I could still see them.

"Hello," I said, sounding a lot braver than I felt. There was something about their energy that put me on edge. "Did you need something?"

My question was met with stoic silence, and I noticed that the entire area around us had fallen completely silent—no leaves rustling, no birds singing, and no squirrels scurrying along the ground or through the trees.

"I can see you, you know," I said, turning slowly around, trying to keep track of how many dark shadows were around me. I counted three.

Because they stayed a couple hundred feet away from me and were partially concealed by trees and tombstones, I couldn't distinguish whether they were spirits or shadow people, but one thing I knew for sure: they were starting to make me really uncomfortable.

Their energy didn't feel threatening, but then again, I could only sense the energy from that distance, and not well enough to get a good read on their intentions, unless I could lure them closer—something I wasn't sure I wanted to do. Yet I couldn't stand here all day waiting for their next move, either.

"Okay," I thought, "if they're shadow people, they should scurry away if I approach them. Let's see what happens."

Squaring my shoulders, I purposely started to walk toward one of the dark shadows. As soon as I got a little closer, I could sense that they were spirits, not shadow people.

Judging by their energy, I could sense they were male. However, their vague outlines made it impossible to distinguish any other identifying characteristics.

"Do you need help?" I asked. In response, one of the spirits simply disappeared and the rest of his companions quickly followed.

"Interesting," I said. As I trudged back over to the family plot, I thought, *I wonder if they're some of my relatives. Why wouldn't they communicate with me?*

After gathering my things, I drove back up to the cemetery office to pick up the copies the clerk made for me.

The clerk, a middle-aged woman with short blond hair, a friendly face, and clear blue eyes, greeted me enthusiastically when I walked into the office.

"How'd your research go?" she asked, carefully sliding my copies into a large manila envelope.

"Great, thanks."

"I'm Sherry, by the way."

"Debi. It's nice to meet you," I said, shaking her hand across the counter.

"You from around here? I haven't seen you before," Sherry said, casting an openly curious glance my way.

"No. Michigan. I'm just out here doing some family research," I said.

"Where you staying?"

"Don't know yet. Probably one of the hotels close to town," I shrugged.

"I'd recommend one of the big chain hotels," Sherry said quietly, giving me a knowing look. "My husband Rob and I just moved here about six months ago. We got hired on as caretakers for the cemetery. We live in the house next door." She tilted her head to the right.

"How nice. It's really pretty here," I responded politely.

"It is," Sherry admitted, as she started to re-file the burial cards and other information she'd copied for me. "But it takes a while to get accepted by the townsfolk around here, I guess."

I got the feeling Sherry was kind of lonely and needed a friend. I saw my opportunity.

"Listen, this may sound strange, but have there been any reports of ghosts in the cemetery since you've been here?" I asked.

Sherry stopped what she was doing and froze in place. I saw a trace of fear flash over her face and quickly disappear.

"Why? What happened?" she asked warily, not meeting my eyes.

"Look, Sherry, it's okay, you can tell me. I'm a ghost hunter. I'm used to dealing with these things," I assured her.

She visibly relaxed, and tucked a piece of stray blond hair behind her ear before speaking.

"Listen, let's go get you checked into a hotel and we'll go get something to eat. Rob's on a fishing trip this weekend. I'll tell you all about it over dinner. It's just about closing time anyway," Sherry said.

"Sounds good to me," I agreed.

I waited patiently while Sherry locked up the office, and then I followed her into town. She pulled into a local chain motel. After registering, I put my suitcases upstairs before rejoining Sherry in her Ford Bronco. We drove to a local restaurant and sat down in a booth in the back.

After ordering, I decided to press Sherry about the cemetery.

"So, tell me about the cemetery," I said, taking a sip of my Diet Coke.

"There are shadows," Sherry began. "They show up a lot and are scaring away mourners and people visiting gravesites. I've seen them once myself. There doesn't seem to be any rhyme or reason to whom they appear to, nor when they show up. It's to the point I won't even go through the cemetery by myself. I'm so scared."

"I saw them," I said. "They don't appear to be threatening. Any idea why they're there?"

"No. I wish I knew," Sherry said wistfully.

"Have you called in a team of paranormal investigators?" I asked.

The waitress delivered our food, so it took a moment for Sherry to answer.

"No. I don't want people to think I'm nuts, and I wouldn't even know who to call anyway. I mean, if word got around that the cemetery was haunted…" she said, taking a bite of her pasta.

"Sherry, since other people have seen them, I'm pretty sure a lot of people know the cemetery is haunted. But, maybe I can find out what they want and put a stop to this. They really need to be crossed over," I told her. "Why don't you come back to the cemetery with me? We'll do a little nighttime investigation and maybe figure this whole thing out."

"No way am I going into that cemetery at night. It's creepy enough during the day," Sherry said, emphatically slamming her fork down on her plate.

"Okay, okay," I laughed, wiping my mouth with my napkin. "Let me into the cemetery tonight and I'll see what I can do."

"By yourself?" Sherry asked, her eyes growing wide.

"Yes. Not the safest way to investigate, but since you won't come with me ..." I shrugged.

"I'll come with you," Sherry sighed. "But only if I can wait in the car so I can go for help if something happens."

"Deal," I agreed.

We continued to talk over dinner about ghost hunting and what I was going to do later that night. She dropped me back at the hotel and we agreed to meet at the cemetery gates around ten o'clock that night.

Cursing myself for not bringing any ghost hunting equipment with me, I drove to the drugstore—the only shop open in town. I quickly discovered I was going to have to conduct an old-school ghost hunt, because all I could find was a microcassette recorder, some tapes, batteries, and a flashlight —I already had my digital camera with me. It wasn't much, but it was all I could muster up on such short notice.

The inky blackness of the night seemed to engulf the entire Jeep on the way back to the cemetery. The moon sat hidden behind ominous dark clouds, and streetlights, once you left the town proper, were few and far between.

The headlights pierced the darkness and illuminated Sherry's car waiting for me just outside the gates. Sherry had already opened the gates and waved me through. I stopped by the office to help her close and lock the massive iron gates to the cemetery behind us.

"Are you sure you want to do this?" she asked, her arms wrapped around her midsection, as if to protect herself from a sudden onset of ghosts.

"I'm sure. Come on. It'll be fun," I said as we walked back to my truck. "Tell me where these ghosts normally appear."

"They've been seen just about everywhere in the cemetery, although at night most of the reports come from people who have seen them by the gates," Sherry said, as she opened the door to my truck. "I can't tell you how many people have knocked on our door telling us they saw a group of people trying to get into the cemetery after hours, but when Rob goes and checks, no one is there."

"Okay, let's start here then," I said.

"What do we do?" Sherry asked, looking around nervously.

"We try to coax them out," I answered, as I loaded batteries and a cassette tape into the recorder.

"Can I wait in the car?" Sherry said.

"If you want," I sighed.

Sherry climbed into the passenger seat of the Jeep and quietly shut the door, while I walked toward the gates of the cemetery. I decided to try an EVP session, so I flipped on the tape recorder.

"Is anyone here?" I asked, letting my energy fan out in all directions, hoping to detect one of the ghosts coming in my direction.

No response.

"No one is here to hurt you. We just want to help you. Can you talk to us?" I asked.

Again, no response, and I didn't feel the presence of a spirit anywhere around me.

After about a half-hour of waiting, I rejoined Sherry in the car.

"Let's head back to the Gates of Salvation section, where they appeared to me," I suggested. "Maybe we'll have more luck there."

Sherry agreed and I began slowly weaving my car back through the narrow roads that snaked through the graveyard. Within a few minutes, we arrived back at the Gates of Salvation.

I grabbed my flashlight and started walking around the area, ending up at the back of a section across the street from the Gates of Salvation.

"That's the oldest section of the cemetery," Sherry yelled to me from the safety of my Jeep.

There were graves everywhere, and many of them dated back to Revolutionary War era. As I walked among the gravestones, I found a small, empty area against the back fence. The flashlight revealed woods on the other side of the fence, and other grave markers lining the fence like soldiers.

"Now that's odd. Why wasn't anyone buried here?" I wondered, panning my flashlight around the area. The beam caught a slight movement close to a tall obelisk monument about twenty feet away from me.

Just as I was about to walk toward the movement, I caught something moving out of the corner of my eye. I slowly turned, and my flashlight caught the same three ghostly figures that appeared to me earlier in the day, as they emerged from behind trees and tombstones and stood in a semi-circle in front of me, still keeping some distance away.

"What are you trying to tell me?" I asked, mostly out of frustration. "You can talk to me, I can hear you."

"We lived. No one will know," one of the ghosts said to me telepathically.

"Why?" I asked.

"We have no markers," the ghost answered. "Behind you."

I turned around and saw the empty plot of land by the fence.

"Are you buried there?" I said.

"Yes. Please help us. We lived."

"I'll help you. I promise," I said.

"Thank you." With those words, the ghosts faded back into the night before I could ask their names.

I made a mental note of the people buried on either side of the empty plots and walked back to my truck to rejoin Sherry, whose eyes were wide open in fright.

"We need to get into the office," I said. "We need to find out who is buried in those graves without tombstones."

"Why?" Sherry asked.

"Because that's why the ghosts are here; they want to be remembered and there are no names on those graves."

We drove back up to the front of the cemetery, and she unlocked the office. After about an hour of searching through the files, burial books, and scouring a detailed map of the cemetery, we were able to discover there were a father and two of his sons buried in the unmarked graves.

The records also showed that the father and his sons died within two months of each other in the mid-1800s, from scarlet fever. My research showed that a horrible bout of scarlet fever did go through the area at that time. Given the fact that the father and sons were farmers, which was listed on the cemetery records, they probably didn't have the money to pay for markers—a sad tale to be sure.

"What do we do know?" Sherry asked.

"We get some sleep. When does Rob come back from fishing?" I asked.

"In the morning, why?" Sherry asked.

"Tell Rob to make some wooden crosses, write the men's names on them and put them at the gravesites. That should take care of your problem," I answered.

After bidding Sherry goodbye, I returned to the hotel for some much-needed sleep. The next morning, I stopped by the cemetery to say goodbye to Sherry and started the long trek home.

Two weeks later I received an e-mail from Sherry saying that since Rob put the crosses at the gravesites, there have been no more sightings of the phantoms. They'd just wanted someone to know they lived and they mattered.

The Cemetery Where Few Rest in Peace

A small cemetery we'll call Palmdale is also one of the exceptions to the norm. The cemetery is located just outside of a small town in Michigan. Due to recent acts of vandalism and the desire to protect the small cemetery, I will not divulge the exact location.

The cemetery itself dates back to the very early 1800s, and there is still the occasional burial taking place even today. The graveyard sits on a heavily wooded, large parcel of land surrounded by residential homes, although I'm sure this wasn't always the case, as most of the houses are relatively new.

Historical records show that at one time there were two Native American reservations within fifteen miles of the cemetery, and five known Native American burial grounds within six miles of the graveyard. It's common knowledge that Native Americans once roamed the land freely, and the location of the cemetery was considered a neutral zone by the area Indian tribes.

Different tribes would come to this area to bury their dead, because of the close proximity to the water. Many Native American tribes in this area buried their dead close to the water because they believed the flow of the water would assist in carrying the soul of the deceased to the other side. The area was rich in fish and game, and many members of several tribes would peacefully hunt, fish, and perform their burial rituals in peace.

Once the area became settled, after the War of 1812, the Brits set up a fort close to the location and the Native Americans were rounded up on the reservations. Different treaties were signed, and eventually many of the members of the various Indian tribes were shipped off to Canada.

Much of this history has long been forgotten, as the bustling town developed into one of the main shipping ports on the Great Lakes. In present day, the town's importance to the shipping industry is gone, and the once-busy docks that moored schooners and other types of shipping vessels have been eroded away by time and the waters of the large lake nearby. Few of the original buildings remain, some destroyed because of the fire that roared through town in the 1870s, and some demolished due to the evolution of a society that demanded larger, more modern facilities. Some of the original buildings, such as two large hotels that burned to the ground in the fire, have never been rebuilt.

Palmdale Cemetery holds the remains of many of the founding fathers of the small Michigan hamlet, which we'll call Ashley, along with a host of settlers and unknown seamen who died while in port, or en route to Ashley.

The cemetery is encircled by a road, and another road leads from the main gates straight to a small white building, with a covered wraparound porch. A bench is built into one side of the building.

On the surface, the cemetery looks like any other old graveyard: rows of tombstones lined up like mismatched soldiers; the brief life stories of the dead carved on the tombstones, showing the dates of birth and death and, in many cases, a small epitaph.

These grave markers all stand as a grim reminder that one day, we too shall leave our earthly bodies and take spirit form. The cemetery itself appears to be a calm, peaceful place for the bodies of the dead, and a good place to reflect and remember the loved ones we've lost to the inevitable clutches of death.

However, if you pay attention and take the time to cut into the underbelly of the cemetery, it's an entirely different story. Many residents of Ashley know about the paranormal side of Palmdale Cemetery. Some have even experienced it firsthand, although rarely, if at all, will they speak of it. Even when they do, it's only with trusted friends and in hushed voices.

On my first visit to Palmdale Cemetery, I too thought it was a serene environment and the entire place seemed rather benign—until I really began to concentrate. I decided to delve a little deeper into the undercurrents of energy that softly pulsated and danced among the tombstones.

I walked down the road toward the white building, and settled myself on the bench that overlooks the western side of the graveyard. My intention was to simply soak in the energy and see what happened. After closing my eyes and taking a few deep breaths to lower my energy vibration to match those in the cemetery, I opened my eyes and sat perfectly still, careful not to let my eyes focus on any one thing, but to see everything all at once.

You know that old saying, "sometimes you can't see the forest for the trees"? That's exactly what happened. When I did take the time to really notice what was around me, I saw that there were dark shadows, roughly in the shape of humans, standing among the trees and tombstones. It was then I noticed that the energy had changed dramatically. It went from barely perceptible to pulsating. The air felt electric and fully charged—not threatening—but definitely pumped up enough to where you couldn't miss it if you tried.

The shadows were making no attempt at contact. I got up off the bench and walked around the building, keeping my eyes peeled for any other shadows. After I completed the rather large circle, it hit me that I was completely surrounded by the shadows.

Feeling rather uneasy about the whole situation, and silently cursing myself for not being more alert, I sat back down on the hard, wooden bench to see what was going to happen next and to think about what to do about the situation I found myself in.

Being surrounded by dark shadows normally isn't a good thing. Due to the fact that they were standing some distance away from me, I couldn't really pick up on their energy enough to determine if they were just curious spirits or malevolent entities, but to tell the truth, while I was very uneasy, I didn't really feel I was in eminent danger.

Fifteen minutes later they hadn't moved, and I was still sitting in the same place as well. We obviously were at a stalemate.

Someone once told me that the best defense is a good offense—must be a football thing. Anyway, that principle applies in almost every life situation, even when you're dealing with the dead.

I got up from the bench and walked to the back of the building. From there, I had a pretty decent view of the entire cemetery and was quickly able to determine there were no other living people in the graveyard—at least that was working in my favor. Seeing a person walking around talking to seemingly nothing tends to raise eyebrows and make parents grab their children and rush away from you. Ah, the life of a psychic medium ...

"I can see all of you," I said, turning around in place to address all the shadows. "I'm not here to harm you in any way and I'm not afraid of you, so you can come forward and tell me what you want."

Nothing—they gave me nothing. I know they heard me, because they glanced back and forth at each other. This told me that they were not shadow people, because shadow people make no attempt to communicate with the living, and once discovered, a shadow person will normally race faster than the speed of light to get away from the living.

This told me they were intelligent entities, very capable of communicating with the living. It also meant that they could probably manipulate objects in their environment, which could spell trouble for me, because they could throw things and move other objects that could cause me harm. There were rocks, heavy urns to hold flowers, large sticks and branches, and pinecones littering the cemetery floor. Any of those could be a weapon of some type that the spirits could use to hurt me.

It wouldn't be the first time I've had something thrown at me or been attacked by a spirit. I've had books, table knives, and other assorted items hurled at me, and I have also been scratched, punched, and shoved by ghosts and other types of entities. I didn't want this situation to get out of control, because in this case I was completely outnumbered.

So far, the whole offense thing wasn't working out the way I'd envisioned, so I decided to step it up a notch.

With a purposeful stride and my hands clenched at my sides, I began to walk toward the shadow spirits directly in front of me. I was careful not to seem aggressive, but rather emit an aura of having a sense of purpose.

This approach seemed to work as the shadow spirits began to move en mass toward the rear of the cemetery before disappearing altogether. Curious, I decided to follow them and walked down the center road, toward the fence at the rear of the graveyard.

Upon arriving at the back of the cemetery, I was met by the spirit of a Native American brave standing on the other side of the fence. His dark skin, long dark hair that held three feathers pointing in a downward direction, his ebony, smoldering eyes, and ruggedly handsome features were striking. Bare-chested and wearing a loin cloth made of subtle deer hide, he stood in stoic silence waiting for me to approach him.

In his left hand, he held a spear adorned with two feathers that had a string of colorful beads securing them to the staff. The spearhead was pointing upright in a non-threatening manner.

Slowing my pace, so as not to startle the spirit, I approached the fence line.

"Hello. Did you need help?" I asked.

"No," the spirit answered telepathically. "I want to show you something."

"Okay," I responded in kind.

The brave turned to the side and waved the spear in a sweeping motion behind him. Immediately in my mind's eye, I saw a Native American encampment where half-built houses now stood. There were many Native Americans carrying on with their daily chores while a large fire burned in the middle of the settlement.

Deer hides were stretched on frames made of sturdy tree branches and were being carefully cleaned. The women were preparing food and gathering wood for the fire, while many of the men were sharpening their spears or making new arrowheads. I saw a thick forest of trees where a field now stands—all the trees cleared to make way for a growing society.

"We were here," the brave told me. "I just wanted you to know."

"I'm deeply honored that you shared this with me," I told him.

"We will see each other again soon. Walk in peace, my friend," the brave said before all that existed in the past, along with the spirit, vanished into thin air, leaving only the subdivision under construction in its wake.

Judging by the encounter with the Native American brave, I can only assume the shadow spirits in the cemetery were Indians, however I kind of doubt it because the energy felt different than that of the Native American man.

To this day, the shadow spirits appear day and night in the cemetery, however I've had no further contact with the handsome brave or any of his tribe since that time. I often wonder what the real purpose of the Native American spirit was, when he showed me the settlement that once stood there. Could he have been a spirit guide trying to reassure me? Or, alternatively, did he just appear, like so many other ghosts and spirits do, because he knew I could see and communicate with him? I may never know, but I'm grateful for the moment we shared.

Fascinated by this experience, I became curious as to what other activity may be present at the cemetery. I called in my paranormal investigation team, and we spent several nights in the cemetery.

Our tape recorders picked up many EVPs that included spirits asking for help, the laughter of children, and one heart-wrenching EVP of a little girl who asked if we were going to leave her there alone. Unfortunately, I was in a different part of the cemetery when the EVP was recorded and didn't hear the little girl's voice until we reviewed the tapes a few days later. I went back to the cemetery in an attempt to communicate with her. I found her gravesite, but couldn't find her gentle spirit.

One clear, chilly autumn night, the team went to the cemetery to conduct further investigations. Crisp leaves littered the ground, and a bright moon cast barely enough light to safely navigate the cemetery without the use of a flashlight, casting eerie shadows across the tombstones and ground.

The team divided into pairs, and each took off in their own direction to investigate different parts of the sprawling cemetery.

One of the team members and I headed up toward the front of the cemetery to investigate the area by the cemetery gates. As we walked, leaves crunched under our feet. We then noticed that we could hear another set of footsteps besides our own. They seemed to be coming from behind a row of tall lilac bushes that lay directly to our left.

We stopped and turned around to see if any of our fellow team members were in the area. As soon as we stopped, we heard the other set of footsteps take two or three more steps before ceasing. There were no other team members remotely close to where we were.

"Is anyone there?" I called out into the dimly lit cemetery. No response.

My teammate walked over to the lilac bushes and peeked behind them to see if anyone was playing a trick on us, but there wasn't a living soul to be found. I quickly looked around to see if there were any of the now familiar shadow spirits around, but there weren't.

Shrugging our shoulders, we continued our journey toward the front gate. Again we heard the sound of footprints walking alongside us, but a short distance away. We were definitely being followed by an unseen entity.

Once we reached our destination, I turned around and scanned the entire cemetery to see if I could find out where our other team members were. I saw the bobbing of their flashlights, and the flash of digital cameras in different areas of the graveyard, but none within close proximity to our location.

Once again the footsteps had stopped, but I was picking up a small concentration of energy from the front gates, the exact area the phantom footsteps came from.

"I know you're there," I announced. "I can feel your energy. Make your presence known."

A few seconds later a white, ectoplasm mist began to form in front of the gates, in the vague outline of a person. My teammate began to snap a few pictures, while I continued to try to make contact with this unknown entity.

"Who are you?" I asked telepathically.

"The gatekeeper," the spirit replied. "What are all these people doing here?"

"Looking for you," I giggled. "We mean no harm."

"I understand. Carry on, but I will be watching," the spirit replied and then dissipated into nothingness.

The remainder of that night in the cemetery was uneventful. However, a few nights later a friend of mine and I were in the cemetery in the wee hours of the morning, taking pictures.

As we slowly drove toward the front gate to leave, we saw two men dressed in work clothes shut the gate, cutting off our only exit! The men then walked down the sidewalk by the main road, and when they got under a street light they simply vanished.

My friend stopped her truck and we both looked at each other mystified. I jumped out of the vehicle and approached the gates.

The heavy chain that held the two gates together was draped through both wrought-iron gates, but thankfully wasn't locked. I unwound the chain and opened the gates so my friend could pull out of the cemetery. I then shut the gates, replaced the chain, and walked over to where my friend was parked by the side of the road.

I never saw the two spectral workmen again, and we haven't quite decided if the workmen were shutting the gate to keep us in, or if they were even aware of our presence.

It's totally possible that the workmen were simply residual energy and not ghosts at all. The energy of something repetitious, such as locking a gate every night, could replay itself over and over like a video tape.

Palmdale Cemetery seems to be evolving in some mysterious way. Every time we go there, something new and exciting happens; however, a few things do remain constant.

The shadow spirits will appear and, at a discreet distance away, surround you before you even realize what happened. Around a few certain graves you will hear children laughing and dancing, like they're playing a game. On a really good night, if you're taking pictures, the guardian of the gate will appear in mist form in some of the pictures and, if you're lucky, you will get a picture of him bowing a greeting your way.

I've yet to hear any stories or experience anything menacing or threatening. That could change though. A ghost hunting excursion to Palmdale Cemetery is always unpredictable. However, the city has stopped allowing people, even ghost hunting teams, into the cemetery at night, due to vandalism. Who knows what else is happening there now?

I have been there several times recently during the daylight hours, and have experienced some paranormal activity that includes footsteps following me, shadow spirits darting in and out among the trees and grave markers, and, occasionally, the sound of the children playing.

Just a few months ago, I caught wind, through the words of a friend, that someone had gone into the cemetery and dumped salt around a young woman's grave. This young woman died in 1881, and I've met her ghost on several occasions while investigating the house she once lived in.

The only reason you would surround a grave, or anything for that matter, with salt is to keep an evil spirit or demon from crossing over the line of salt and roaming free.

To put salt around a grave would prevent the spirit, if malevolent, from being able to move beyond that point. I can speak from experience and would swear that the young woman in that grave is one of the kindest, gentlest souls I've ever met—living or dead, and would do nothing to harm a living human being. The rain and snow have washed away the salt, so her spirit can once again be free; honestly, I'm a little concerned for her, as I haven't seen her spirit since this incident.

Personally I've never put sea salt around a grave for any reason, nor have I heard of anyone in the paranormal field that has done so either, however that doesn't mean it hasn't happened.

So, the mystique of Palmdale Cemetery lives on. Some of the people who died many years ago are not resting in peace and, in some cases, the living aren't allowing them to.

Chapter 11

The Haunted Church

Now, I know you're thinking, "Churches are haunted? Aren't they supposed to be sacred places?" They are sacred places, and that's exactly why they're haunted, although not many churches will admit to it.

According to some pastors I've spoken with, they are constantly trying to keep dark energies out of their churches. I'm not sure if they mean that literally or figuratively, but the fact remains there is a spiritual warfare battle taking place right under many people's noses, and they don't even realize it—which is probably for the best in some cases.

One of the reverends I've spoken to in the past, but who is not related to the following story, told me that their church fell victim to a demonic entity at one time, and it took a lot of work to get rid of it. I didn't find this out of the realm of possibility, because many people believe that a demon's sole purpose is to try to turn people away from God, and what better place to try to do this than at a church, where you have a lot of people. It kind of goes back to that old saying about killing two birds with one stone. You have a ready audience, all assembled in God's house. There is a lot of irony in a demon coming into a church to turn its parishioners away from the very thing they came there to worship.

Anyway, our team, Black River Paranormal, was called in to investigate some strange happenings at a rather large church nestled in a small hamlet in the Thumb Area of Michigan. Lights were turned on and off with some frequency, and although the electricity in the church had been checked numerous times by electricians, no problems were ever found, and other types of paranormal activity such as footsteps and shadows had been observed.

The church grounds are massive. There are two parking lots—one for Sunday mass and one for the cemetery that lies behind the church.

The original section of the building is adorned by a tall steeple, and also holds the sanctuary, with a balcony that includes seating and the door to the steeple. There is a basement under this part of the church, and the mechanical workings of the church such as the furnace, etc., are housed in a small area, while the rest of the basement contains a pool table and other pieces of furniture. This room's primary purpose is to be the teen center.

The addition to the church was added sometime in the 1960s and holds large classrooms, the church offices, an ample kitchen area, and other rooms used for various purposes, depending on the needs and desires of the parishioners.

When we arrived, the pastor met us at the side door, and seemed relieved that we were there. As I walked through the double doors, I was immediately struck by a wall of energy that tried to push me out of the building. While it didn't feel especially malevolent, it was obvious something or someone didn't want me there. The question was why? Pushing through the energy, I joined the team and the pastor in one of the smaller meeting rooms, and went over what activity they'd been experiencing.

The pastor reported that the teenagers were seeing dark shadows by the pool table downstairs. Also in the basement, there was a small set of stairs that lead to a door to the outside. This is located right by the furnace room. People have seen a shadow come out of the furnace room, and they watched it walk up the few stairs and through the door. When this happened, footfalls could be heard on the concrete steps.

In other parts of the building, lights would turn on and off at will and various objects were being rearranged in the sanctuary and other rooms, although nothing was being damaged.

The pastor also reported that her own son saw a man walk out of the cemetery and come up to the double doors on that side of the building. The man then attempted to open the doors, which were locked at the time, and he shook them violently.

When the pastor's son walked over to the doors, to see what the man wanted and if he needed help, the man vanished before his very eyes. Obviously, this was very startling for the young man, who immediately ran through the church to tell his mom.

After the client interview, most of the team returned to their vehicles to retrieve the equipment. Randy and I decided to do a walk-through of the entire building to get a sense of where any ghosts or spirits were, so we'd know where to set up our static cameras and let them run during the investigation of the building and church cemetery.

We decided to start in the basement, since that appeared to be where most of the activity was taking place, and then work our way through the building one room at a time.

Upon entering the basement area, I immediately picked up on the presence of a male spirit over by the furnace room. His energy was not threatening, and it felt like he belonged there in some capacity. Making a mental note to revisit this area later in the evening to conduct a more thorough investigation, we made our way up to the main floor of the church. While the energy of the spirit of the man by the furnace room was strong, it didn't feel particularly menacing, just more protective over the church.

The kitchen and office areas were unremarkable, so we knew we wouldn't have to spend much time in those areas later.

We then turned our attention to the sanctuary, which consumed most of the first floor. Rows of pews, with aisles on either side and down the center, stood at the ready to welcome people for Sunday service. The vaulted ceiling was at least two stories tall, making the room look twice the size it really was.

Two sets of narrow steps with white railings led up to the balcony area to the rear of the sanctuary. Randy and I made our way up one set of staircases, and we noticed the door to the steeple was set behind the balcony seating area. A narrow aisle separated the balcony seats from the steeple door.

As I reached for the doorknob to open the door to the steeple, Randy and I both heard a distinct low, throaty growl come from behind the other side of the door! I immediately jerked my hand back from the doorknob.

"That was interesting. What do you think that was?" Randy asked.

"I'm not sure yet," I shrugged, and once again grasped the doorknob and opened the door. There was a very small room with shelves on both sides that, at the moment, was used to store church items that weren't often needed.

Randy and I both peered up the center of the room to the top of the steeple. Nothing seemed amiss, and I wasn't picking up any discernible energy coming from the space. Whatever growled at us a few seconds before was nowhere to be found!

When we came down from the balcony, we discovered the rest of the team was set up and ready to go. We directed our tech manager to put the cameras in the balcony of the sanctuary and in the basement area, being sure to capture not only the pool table, but the stairway next to the furnace room that led outside, as well.

With all the equipment in place, and the team members divided into pairs, we turned off all the lights and started investigating.

Randy, the pastor, and I walked into one of the large meeting rooms. I'd detected a presence in there earlier and wanted to find out who it was. This spirit's energy was different from the man in the basement, and I was curious as to who he was. I didn't have to wait long. Once I opened myself up to receive the energy, the spirit made contact.

"Who are you?" I asked aloud.

"Samuel," the spirit replied telepathically.

"Hi, Samuel, I'm Debi. We're not here to harm you in any way. Why are you in the church?"

"I used to come to church here."

In my mind I saw a short, older man with a bald head. His hands were calloused from work and his entire demeanor was one of humility. I described the man to the pastor. She didn't recognize the name or the description of the man, but said he could have been here before she became pastor.

"Did you spend a lot of time here?" I asked. Spirits generally will return to a place they loved, or were the most content in, when they were alive.

"I took care of the grounds and the flower beds," Samuel said with pride in his voice.

"I'm sure you did a great job. Why are you still here? Do you know you've died?"

"Yes, I'm aware that my body died, but I really don't have any place else I'd rather be. I loved working around here. I'm buried in the cemetery out back," he volunteered.

"It's a beautiful place to be buried," I agreed. "Did you need help with something? Have you crossed over?"

"Yes, I went into the light; it's beautiful there, but I wanted to come back and make sure the church was okay. Do you know there's another one like me in the basement? I don't think he likes me very much," Samuel fretted. "Course, then again I don't care for him too much either."

"Why's that?"

"He keeps trying to do my job. We argue a lot. I'm sure he's not a bad person. I mean he's in the church, right? But, if you could try to work out an arrangement with him, where I will stay in this area of the building, and he stays in his, I'd sure appreciate it," Samuel said.

"I'll see what I can do. Thanks, Samuel." I concluded the conversation with the spirit and decided to tackle the basement next.

As Randy, the pastor, and I walked through the building toward the basement stairs, we talked about Samuel, and the pastor said she'd look at the cemetery records to see if we could find out more about him. I sent her off to do that, and Randy and I proceeded down to the basement area.

The air in the basement felt heavier and thicker than in any of the other areas of the church, an atmosphere that wasn't present the first time I was in the basement. This told me that there was either some type of dark entity, or a rather powerful spirit who occupied this space. Since Samuel told me that the spirit in the basement was a man, I had to assume, until further notice, that we were dealing with a normal spirit, and not anything demonic. My first thought was that the spirit I'd noticed in the basement earlier was beginning to feel threatened by our presence.

I made my way over to the furnace room with Randy and his video camera in tow. Immediately, I could sense a male spirit that wanted to make contact.

"Who are you?" I asked.

"I worked at the church," the spirit answered.

"That's funny. That's what the guy upstairs said," I quipped.

"Maybe, but I'm the real caretaker," the spirit insisted.

"Okay, look. Is it possible that both of you worked at the church, but at different times, and probably different eras?" I asked.

"It's possible, I suppose," the spirit begrudgingly admitted.

"Are you the one who scares the kids and appears as a dark shadow by the pool table?" I said.

"Yes, that's me. Darn kids are so loud sometimes. I do it to quiet them down," he admitted sheepishly.

"Will you show yourself to me, please?" I said. In my mind's eye, I saw a big burly man with ruddy skin and kind blue eyes. His hands were massive, and he had to have stood well over six feet tall. His light brown hair was bushy, and he was wearing work clothes from the middle- to late-1800s. Now things were beginning to make sense.

When I saw Samuel, he was wearing work clothes from the mid- to late-1940s. I took the time to explain this to the spirit, and asked him to please not scare the teenagers anymore. I also told him that I would talk to Samuel and ask him to stay in the newer part of the church, while this spirit must remain in the original section of the building. The spirit agreed.

During the time I was working out this arrangement with the spirit, Randy was videotaping everything, and said he could see the shadow of a large man on the staircase leading from the furnace room to the outdoors. This confirmed that Randy and I were seeing the same spirit. Although Randy isn't a medium, nor accustomed to seeing spirits, every once in a while a spirit will put an image of itself in his head, or show themselves to him in some way.

Randy and I left the basement and worked our way back upstairs to see how the rest of the team was making out. As we passed by the office area, the pastor stopped us and said that she'd found a Samuel buried in the cemetery, and gave us the location.

Gathering the team together, we left the church and turned our attention to the cemetery. I gave the rest of the team Samuel's name and approximate location of his grave, and we fanned out in search of his burial place.

We finally located his tombstone under a tree in the middle of the cemetery. This at least confirmed that a man named Samuel was a member of the congregation at one time and had died in the early 1950s.

Many of the team members spent a great deal of time in the sanctuary balcony, trying to debunk the growl Randy and I heard. They tried everything they could think of, from listening to passing cars and trucks, walking across different parts of the old, worn, wood floor, etc. They even conducted a complete search of the steeple room and the rest of the building, looking for any type of animal that could have made the noise. They reported that they didn't even find any signs that an animal had ever been in any part of the church. And they couldn't duplicate the noise, or explain why the growl was heard in the first place.

This made me a little uneasy. It meant that there could possibly be some type of inhuman entity present in the church. Randy and I spent the better part of two hours conducting EVP sessions, taking pictures, and reaching out asking the being to identify itself. No matter what we tried, we were met with total silence. Even upon playback of the audio, nothing was heard that we couldn't explain.

Around two o'clock in the morning, I decided to call it a night. The rest of the team wanted to stay later and do more investigation. I bid everyone a good night and got in my car to leave.

As I pulled away, I happened to glance up at the steeple, brightly lit by flood lamps. There, at the very top, I would swear, even now, that there was an impish demon hanging onto the top of the steeple looking right at me, in a mocking manner.

I called Randy on his cellphone and told him what I'd seen. The next day, he telephoned to say they were at the site until about four o'clock in the morning, but they found no sign of the demon I'd seen.

Last time we checked, the pastor reported that things have calmed down considerably. No longer are the teenagers being frightened by a dark shadow, and items are remaining in place. Still, I have to wonder if somewhere, waiting for the right opportunity, the demon I saw is waiting to strike—only time will tell.

Chapter 12

HOME SWEET HAUNTED HOME

While it's not unusual for the owner of a house to haunt the place after they die, every once in a while you come across a very unique case. The Loop-Harrison mansion is one of those cases. The house was built in the 1800s, and the people who have lived there throughout the years have retained almost every object from previous owners. This not only preserved history, it also left a multitude of objects for spirits to come back and live in after death.

Close to the tip of the Thumb Area in the State of Michigan stands a glorious mansion. It's built in the style of a house that looks like it appeared in the movie *Mary Poppins*—a large Elizabethan mansion that is absolutely gorgeous.

Dr. Loop, a country doctor, built the home for his adoring wife in the 1800s. Together they raised two children, Emma and Stanley, in the home. The good doctor added a side entrance that led directly into his office, where he would see his patients.

History tells us that Dr. Loop performed more than one surgery on the massive, wooden kitchen table, and that not all of his patients lived through their operations.

The house itself is three stories tall; the third story constitutes the attic. It sits on ten acres of property that now is home to many historic buildings that have been moved there from their previous locations. The original barn Dr. Loop built is now home to a very popular community theatre.

What's even more remarkable is that the Loop family threw little away. Most of the original furniture and all of Dr. Loop's medical records, medicine, and surgical instruments remain in the house to this day.

Dr. Loop's son, Stanley, joined the military and quickly rose to the rank of captain. His daughter, Emma, married a minister, and they lived in the home with Dr. Loop and his wife. Once Emma's parents passed away, Emma remained in the home with her husband and children.

Across the street from the Loop family home stood rental properties built by Dr. Loop and owned by the family after the doctor's death. Every month, Emma would dutifully walk across the street and collect the rent from the tenants and check on the property.

One fateful night in the early 1900s, Emma left the mansion and began her walk through the front gardens to the road. She was going to collect the rent money. As she was crossing the road, she was struck by a car.

People rushed to her aid and carried her into one of the parlors of the mansion, and a doctor was summoned. Despite all best efforts, Emma died within a few short hours after the accident. She was buried in the local cemetery, close to her parents.

Years passed, and the house never left the ownership of the family, until one of Emma's relatives deeded the house and property to the city. The city turned the house into a museum, and the rest, as they say, is history.

Since that time, a group of dedicated volunteers have turned the Loop estate in a marvelous place to visit. They've added Native American displays, shipwreck relics, and mementos from every war.

In addition, they've raised money and moved countless historical buildings set for destruction to the property, and these buildings have been lovingly restored and filled with various antiques.

Through all of this, one thing has remained constant: some members of the Loop family aren't ready to give up their home and still roam its halls in spirit.

Our team, Black River Paranormal, was called in to investigate the museum by members of the Board of Directors.

The woman who met with us said that there'd been many reports of Emma being seen in various places around the museum, as well as other paranormal events. The volunteers at the museum wanted to make sure there weren't any malevolent entities, along with Emma, roaming the halls of the house and outbuildings.

One of the volunteers took us out to a small barn behind the house. Inside the barn was an old horse-drawn hearse, complete with the basket Dr. Loop used to put the bodies in for transport! While no one has admitted to any paranormal activity in the area around the hearse, I wouldn't be a bit surprised if some was occurring.

The hearse was black, of course, and held lanterns on the seat on either side of the driver's bench and, if memory serves me correctly, lanterns on the rear of the vehicle as well.

We were mesmerized by the look and feeling of the hearse. The energy around the hearse didn't feel odd, although I did detect an air of sadness, which wouldn't be unusual. The museum volunteer opened the back doors of the hearse so we could climb up the steps attached to the hearse and look inside. We climbed up the back and stuck our heads inside of it to get a closer look. We could still detect the sweet, sickly smell of death permeating from the basket and inside walls. The hearse was way too cool! All of use wanted to stay to see if any spirits lingered within its eerie interior, but, alas, the mansion beckoned and we were anxious to get the investigation going.

The team and some of the volunteers gathered around the massive, well-worn wooden table in the kitchen—the same one Dr. Loop used to perform surgeries on, and on which many people died.

Donna, as we'll call her, told us that Emma seems to be the most active in the house. She told us that one time, during a party, one of the guests felt someone take his arm.

When he turned around to see who it was, there was no one even near him at the time.

On another occasion, one of the volunteers saw Emma standing at the top of the stairs. She appeared to be watching people decorate the house for Christmas, with many of the antique tree ornaments and other holiday decorations Emma would have used during her lifetime. When Emma realized she'd been discovered, she completely vanished right before the person's eyes.

Donna went on to tell us about a recent event in which the fire inspector came to check the fire extinguishers, and make sure the museum met all fire safety standards.

He climbed the stairs to the second floor and turned the corner toward the long hallway that ran the length of the house. He went into the first room on the right, which would have been Emma's room. He saw a woman standing in front of the window on the other side of the room.

She was dressed in period clothing from the late 1800s to early 1900s, and the fire inspector assumed it was one of the volunteers dressed in clothing to match the era of the home—that is until he realized the woman didn't have any feet, and appeared to be suspended in mid-air!

He was frozen in place with confusion and fear. The woman turned and smiled at him and then dissipated into nothingness. That was enough for the inspector. He raced down the stairs and out of the house, like he'd been shot from a cannon.

One of the museum volunteers ran out after him, and the inspector told her what he'd experienced. She coaxed him back into the house and showed him a picture of Emma. The fire inspector confirmed she was the woman he'd seen.

Captain Stanley's room, which is down the hall to the left, holds not only some of the captain's own personal items, but items from various shipwrecks, including the *Regina*. The *Regina* sunk on Lake Huron, close to where the museum is located.

Donna reported that numerous people, including herself, have seen a man looking out the back window of the room. People have seen the curtain pulled back, and the distinct features of a man's face watching them from above. Whether this man is Captain Stanley or not is uncertain, because the features of the man appear distorted due to the original glass, which is kind of wavy, and the fact that the spirit probably wasn't fully materializing.

She went on to say that medicinal odors have been detected on many occasions in Dr. Loop's office. Upon inspection, we noticed a large cupboard on one of the side walls, filled with medicine bottles that Dr. Loop once used. Some of the bottles still contained medicine. We made a note to try to debunk the odors during the investigation.

There have also been reports of various knickknacks being moved from room to room but, because of the number of volunteers in and out of the museum, it's hard to attribute that activity to anything paranormal.

While some team members set up our wireless cameras and checked other equipment to make sure they were functional and had fresh batteries, I wandered into Dr. Loop's office, which is just out the kitchen door, to the left.

Sitting in a chair behind the desk was a life-sized mannequin, with a head that was fashioned to look like Dr. Loop. I have to admit that, number one, I don't like dolls, and number two, this mannequin was just creepy. As you walked around the room, you'd swear the eyes were following you. The entire room had an uneasy feeling about it.

Donna, who'd followed me into the office, told me that sometimes she'd lock up the museum at night, and when she returned the next morning, the mannequin of Dr. Loop would be moved or reposed in some fashion.

While Donna admitted other people have keys to the museum, and that it's possible someone came in after she left late at night and moved the mannequin, she wasn't convinced that was the case. More than once she'd questioned the volunteers after such an event, and they denied being at the museum at all that day.

From a paranormal investigation point of view, we can't attribute Dr. Loop's mannequin moving as a paranormal occurrence, however, we did make sure we had a static video camera pointed at the mannequin the entire time, during the investigation.

With all the equipment in place, the team divided into pairs and headed off to separate areas of the museum. Randy and I decided to start in Dr. Loop's office on the first floor.

We were busy taking pictures and conducting an EVP session, when both of us smelled a very distinctive odor throughout the small room. It was a medicinal smell, but not knowing enough about medications, I couldn't identify what kind.

Randy and I walked over to the medicine cabinet to see if the odor was stronger in that area, but it smelled the same. We then noticed there was a heating vent on the wall next to the medicine cabinet and thought that the aroma of the medicine in the cabinet could be distributed throughout the room when the heat came on.

We requested that the heat be turned off until further notice and then turned on the ceiling fan in the room in an attempt to dissipate the odor. While we were waiting, we walked into the parlor just off of Dr. Loop's office.

This was the lady's parlor, as we'd been told. It held a beautifully upholstered love seat and three matching chairs. The room also contained an old piano that belonged to Emma, and a few end tables.

We spent about an hour investigating that room, with no discernible results, before going back to Dr. Loop's office. The smell we noticed earlier was gone, and we once again began investigating.

Within a few moments, the odor returned—stronger this time. An inspection of the heat vent showed that it was off, and so we turned off the ceiling fan, to see if that made a difference. Once again, we had to wait for the smell to go away, so we went into the gentlemen's parlor to investigate. This room was unremarkable, and yielded nothing paranormal that we could detect.

Randy and I then returned to Dr. Loop's office, and there wasn't any trace of the smell we'd notice before. Again, a few minutes later, the smell returned. We knew the heat was off, and so was the ceiling fan.

This makes perfect sense. It's not unusual for ghosts, spirits, and other types of entities to use a distinct smell to let people know they are there. Granted, this is the first time I'd had a ghost use medicine instead of perfume, tobacco, or flowers, but given that Dr. Loop was a physician, the use of a medicinal odor would distinguish him from any other entity that may be present.

I could sense the presence of a spirit this time, and knew it was a male entity, but every attempt to communicate with him was met with silence. Randy was busy doing an EVP session, and upon playback, we could hear a male voice that didn't belong to Randy, or any other male member of the team, but we couldn't make out what he was saying.

Randy and I then opened the medicine cabinet to see if we could determine what medicine we were smelling. After testing five or six different bottles of liquid medicine, we discovered the odor was caused by digitalis—a heart medication.

We don't know if Dr. Loop took this medicine, but we decided after some debate, that Dr. Loop was using the very unique smell of digitals as a signal to the living that he was present in the space.

As we left the office, we noticed one of our investigators in the foyer conducting an EVP session. The investigator said, "Mrs. Loop? You have a lovely home."

As soon as the words were out of his mouth, we saw him jump back—startled.

"What happened?" I asked.

"Someone put their hand on my wrist," he said. "It wasn't a malicious gesture, it was more of a friendly touch."

"Maybe it was Mrs. Loop thanking you for the compliment," Randy suggested. I nodded in agreement.

"Whoever it was, it would indicate that it was an intelligent entity, wouldn't it?" he asked.

"Definitely," Randy and I answered at the same time.

An intelligent entity is a ghost or spirit that interacts with or acknowledges the living in some manner. Touching our investigator's arm would be the act of an intelligent entity.

"I'm going to keep investigating this area," our investigator said.

"Have fun! We're heading upstairs," Randy said as we walked back down the foyer hallway to the massive, regally designed, semicircular staircase.

The first room on the left as you turned the corner at the top of the stairs to go down the hallway, belonged to Dr. and Mrs. Loop. It's a rather small room, with a gorgeous antique bedroom set and two chairs with a table in between them.

A black dress that belonged to Mrs. Loop lay on the bed and a mannequin in the far corner of the room was adorned in another one of Mrs. Loop's Victorian outfits.

Randy and I spent the better part of an hour trying to make contact with the doctor, or Mrs. Loop, as I could feel a distinct female presence, but nothing happened. I felt that the spirit was relatively shy and more curious about what we were doing than in communicating.

We moved on to Emma's bedroom, on the opposite side of the hallway. This was a large room with an antique bedroom suite, several chairs, a dressing table, and an upholstered bench.

There was also a doll carriage in the room, containing what we believed to be one of Emma's dolls, although it's possible it belonged to her daughter.

The energy in this room felt a little thicker and heavier than in the rest of the house we'd explored so far. This could indicate the presence of a spirit. While I could pick up on a female energy in the room, she didn't go out of her way to communicate, but once she warmed up to us, she began to talk to me telepathically.

Randy and I both felt like we were invading her private space, and although we were slightly uncomfortable, we continued to investigate. I explained to her who we were and why we were there, and apologized for the intrusion.

Emma indicated to me telepathically that she had indeed crossed over to the other side, but she loved to visit her home frequently to check on things and reminisce about her life in the house.

She also said that she was thrilled with how the home has been preserved, and with all the new buildings, most of which she remembers seeing when she was alive, that had been added to the property grounds.

When asked about the incident with the fire inspector, Emma laughed and said she really didn't mean to scare him, but the event amused her greatly. I have to admit, I chuckled right along with her. The vision of the fire inspector racing from the mansion was entertaining.

To me, it felt that Emma was beginning to realize and understand the power she has as a spirit, and she was starting to enjoy her time in the afterlife. All I can say to that is: "You go, girl!"

Emma's energy felt light and playful. I didn't feel that her spirit was capable of any type of malicious event, and was simply, from time to time, visiting a place she loved so dearly in life. I also believe she enjoyed interacting with the living, but on her own terms. I really can't blame her for that.

We thanked Emma for her time and moved on to Captain Stanley's room. This rather small room was filled to bursting with maritime relics. Models of ships, shipwreck relics, and other maritime artifacts sat on display, in every available space.

There were a small table and chairs in the center of the room; the table displayed navigational charts of the Great Lakes. Randy and I made ourselves comfortable in the chairs and tried to open a line of communication with Captain Stanley or any other entity that occupied the space.

After sitting in the room for a short period of time, we noticed that the air was becoming thick and heavy. This energy had a different feel than in the other rooms in the house we'd investigated—it felt a little bit menacing and intimidating, and was definitely male.

Randy tried an EVP session, while I reached out psychically, in an effort to make contact with whatever spirit was in the room with us. Both attempts failed.

We then decided to move on to the military room. Large display cases lined two walls and a large display case ran through the middle of the room. At the back of the room, in front of a window that looked out over the backyard, stood a male mannequin dressed in full combat gear.

Directly to the right of the mannequin was a small room filled with glass display cases. These cases held all types of Native American artifacts, and Randy and I spent a considerable amount of time admiring the various relics.

These two rooms felt light and I couldn't detect the presence of any type of entity, which surprised me. I thought that with all the trappings of war in the room, some type of energy would be clinging to them.

Deciding to take a break, we returned to the kitchen to monitor the equipment so that another team could investigate the upstairs. We had brought a couple of rookie investigators with us, thinking this would be a good case for them to train on, and we sent one of our more experienced investigators with them, to instruct them on the investigative techniques we use.

We settled ourselves at the kitchen table and while I watched the camera feeds, Randy started to review the audio from the tape recorder. We could hear the other team moving around the second floor, so we tried to stay as quiet as possible. We'd discovered early on in the investigation that conversations taking place in the kitchen travel through the heating system, and could give false EVP recordings.

After a couple of hours, the team returned to the kitchen from the second floor.

"We're not going back up there," the rookies announced. I glanced at our experienced investigator, who just shrugged.

"Why? What happened?" Randy asked.

"Something was following us down the hallway from Captain Stanley's room. We tried to do an EVP session, but we don't know if we got anything," they said.

"Okay. So why don't you want to go back upstairs?" I asked.

"Because of the things that follows us." They looked at me as if I'd just landed from Mars.

"Well, that kind of experience is what ghost hunters live for," I explained. "What about the event scared you?"

"It felt like it didn't want us there. It was intimidating. Please don't make us go back up there."

"Okay. Why don't you investigate down here, and Randy and I will go back upstairs," I said.

Relief washed over their faces, and they willingly began to investigate the main floor of the mansion. Randy and I grabbed our gear and hotfooted it back up to the second floor.

As soon as we reached the second-floor landing, it became apparent that the energy had changed dramatically. The energy that we'd felt in Captain Stanley's room seemed to ooze out of the walls and permeate every available space.

Randy and I moved from room to room in search of the source of the energy. We did notice that the only room that didn't have this energy was Emma's. Her room remained calm and serene.

"That's curious." Randy shrugged as we left Emma's room and continued our search.

"It is," I agreed. "Either this entity respects Emma, or Emma is keeping the energy at bay somehow."

We spent the better part of two hours trying to find the source of this heavy energy and make contact, but to no avail. Whatever was up there wasn't in a talkative mood. It just wanted us out.

From what I've been told by the people who work in the museum, Captain Stanley was a rather nice man, so I highly doubted he was responsible for the energy that filled the room.

My best guess is that one of the many maritime relics from past shipwrecks and other sources has a ghost attached to it, and it is he who is responsible for the activity in Captain Stanley's old bedroom.

Defeated, we returned to the kitchen to talk to Donna. We told her what we and our team had experienced on the second floor, and asked if any of the volunteers had similar experiences.

She seemed confused by our question, and said that no one had ever said anything about experiencing the type of activity our team fell victim to. Our only conclusion is that we were strangers to the spirits that either reside here or that visit from time to time.

We believe that the spirits were just trying to protect the museum from a perceived threat. This type of behavior by a ghost or spirit is not uncommon. If they love the place they are inhabiting, many types of entities will try to protect that space from people they don't know.

Because the new investigators were spooked by their experiences, and due to the lateness of the hour, we packed up our gear and left. Donna asked us to come back the next weekend to investigate the other historical buildings on the property. We jumped at the chance.

The following weekend, with more experienced paranormal investigators in tow, we returned to the museum grounds. We invited another paranormal investigation team we've worked with in the past to help, because of the sheer size of the investigation. It would have been impossible for us to cover all twelve-plus outbuildings by ourselves.

We were greeted warmly by a small group of the volunteers and a couple members of the Board of Directors. After introductions were made and the small talk was finished, it was time to get down to business. Once again, the museum was kind enough to let us use the kitchen as command central. One of the volunteers unlocked all the outbuildings, including the restroom building, and then retreated to the kitchen to allow us to do our thing.

The tech people from both teams scurried around the property like rabbits, setting up the equipment in as many buildings we had cameras for. They also checked out all the equipment to ensure everything contained fresh batteries and was in good working order.

We then divided into pairs and headed off in opposite directions.

The first place I wanted to investigate was the old church. The church had a rich history. It once was a grocery store, then a bar, and then a church. The steeple had been added at that point.

Our team usually conducted ghost hunting lectures in the church every October, as a fund-raiser for a museum. It seemed to us, and many of the people present during those lectures, that we weren't alone. We'd done fund-raising lectures for the museum in this building several times before, but this was the first time we'd been able to investigate the grounds and all the outbuildings.

This is because we seemed to always have equipment malfunctions or other type of activity happen during one of our lectures.

Randy and I entered the old church and immediately walked down the center aisle of pews to the raised altar area. To us, this seemed to be the place where much of the activity occurred during the lectures.

We spent a good hour and a half trying to make contact with any entity that may have been present in the church, but all we got in response to our questions were a few odd noises that we couldn't positively attribute to anything paranormal.

As we walked out of the church and headed over to the dairy barn, we heard a scream come from the area where the old train depot stood. Randy and I rushed over to see what happened.

We found a couple of our investigators, along with an investigator from the team we brought along, laughing hysterically. When Larry, one of our investigators could stop laughing long enough, he told us that when Dan, his investigating partner, looked in the window of the train depot, he saw a man sitting at the depot desk. It scared the crap out of him, which is why he screamed. Larry looked in the window and saw that it was a mannequin dressed up as the depot master—hence, the hysterical laughter. This was really a rookie mistake, and happens a lot when someone is amped up to see a ghost and spots a mannequin, or a shadow cast on a wall by some object in the room, etc.

Embarrassed, Larry said it wouldn't happen again, and the team walked around the building to enter the depot. Still chuckling, Randy and I headed back toward the dairy barn.

The dairy barn was filled to overflowing with various equipment that would have been used back in the day. There were old-fashioned milking machines, milk cans, and other paraphernalia. Two narrow mangers lined both sides of the barn and large dairy machines ran down the middle of the building. No one had ever reported anything even remotely paranormal occurring in the dairy barn, but a good paranormal investigator leaves no stone unturned—just in case.

With no activity after a half-hour, Randy and I walked through the property to the old hunting cabin, which sat nestled just inside the tree line on the northern side of the property. A mown trail wound its way a short distance into the woods, toward the cabin.

We first walked around the outside of the cabin to get the lay of the land, and to inspect the building for any holes or unstable beams, and to make sure all the windows were intact. We also checked to see if any tree branches could scrape the sides of roof of the cabin, if the wind blew. That way, if we heard something, we would know whether it was paranormal or caused by the old building itself.

Randy and I climbed the two wooden stairs to the front door and opened it, peering into pitch blackness. The door emitted an eerie creak as it swung open for us to enter. It was so stereotypical of a Hollywood haunted house movie that we both laughed.

Randy and I had no idea, nor did the museum, who all the occupants of the cabin were, over the years, and there'd been no paranormal activity reported, yet that seemed to make the adventure more exciting.

The cabin was so dark, we couldn't see our hands in front of our faces. Even the dim light of the moon coming through the faded curtains did little to pierce the inky blackness that greeted us.

We turned on our UV flashlights, which emitted a soft purplish glow, and we could make out a bunk bed in the far corner of the small cabin and little else. We settled in on the floor and began an EVP session.

At first our questions were met with silence, but as we kept going, we could hear soft taps on the hand-hewn logs of the cabin. We knew there was nothing outside that could cause such noises, but the more we asked questions, the less of a response we got, so we moved on to another building.

We investigated throughout the night, and other than a few inexplicable noises, we didn't receive anything else of note.

We concluded that most of the activity was in the mansion itself, and we plan on revisiting the mansion in the coming months.

As far as Black River Paranormal is concerned, this case is still open and is an ongoing investigation.

While we're in touch with the museum personnel quite a bit during the year, they haven't told us of any other paranormal activity occurring, but that's not unusual. Generally, they save it up for when we are going there to do an investigation and lay it on us all at once—which works out just fine for us.

Chapter 13

WHEN DARKNESS COMES TO PLAY

"It's coming. Can you feel it?" I asked Randy, the founder of Black River Paranormal, who was standing beside me.

"I feel it." Randy scanned the inky black basement of our client's home with the video camera.

My heart felt like it was going to pound out of my chest, as I felt the dark energy come toward us with the power of a freight train.

"I just need it to get a little closer so I can be sure." I took a couple of steps backward until I felt the cold cinder block wall of the basement pressed against my spine.

"Gotcha," Randy whispered.

I shined the beam of my flashlight toward a small opening in the fieldstone wall opposite us. For a brief second, we saw the shadow of an entity peek at out at us before vanishing.

"Let's get back upstairs. I've seen enough," I said, working my way out of the tiny room toward the staircase that led out of the basement and to the light of day. Randy and I both collapsed on the grass when we reached the safety of the outdoors.

"Demonic?" Randy turned off his video camera and exhaled a sigh of resignation.

"Can't say for sure, but it's definitely a negative entity. Let's go talk to the client." I stood up and brushed the loose grass from my jeans.

Even before we pulled into the driveway of our client's house, we both knew it would end up this way. Over the last couple years, Black River Paranormal had gained a reputation as being one of the only paranormal investigation teams in the area that would take on a case dealing with a dark entity. This was just another one to add to the ever-growing list.

Our client, Jennifer (not her real name), and her two teenage daughters lived in the mid-1800s house on a large tract of land out in the middle of nowhere. Jennifer contacted us because of an abundance of paranormal activity occurring in their home.

What sucked us in was the fact that her youngest daughter appeared to be the target of whatever dark entity had taken up residence in the basement.

There had been reports of people being pushed, scratched, and terrorized by this entity, and it was up to us to figure out how to get rid of it. In addition, the family reported seeing the apparition of a man in the barn, apparitions in Jennifer's bedroom, and various apparitions roaming the property. Objects would be moved or thrown around the house, and the paranormal activity was escalating at an alarming rate.

During our various interviews with the client, we learned her ex-husband was deceased, and during his life had been prone to domestic violence. It was our theory that the domestic violence was the catalyst that may have drawn in a demonic entity, which then took up residence in the basement of the house. Not an unusual occurrence, but anytime a possible demonic entity is involved, it makes any situation that much more dangerous to the clients and to our team.

Alternatively, our client's ex-husband could be the malevolent entity in the basement. Either way, our main goal was to protect the safety of our team and our client.

The only other option was that we were dealing with a particularly nasty poltergeist, or the activity was manifesting itself as a poltergeist, because there was a teenager in the house.

It's been a long-standing theory in the paranormal community that oftentimes, if a teenager is present, poltergeist activity could occur. This is due to the fact that the teenager is going through many changes at this time in their life. Their hormones are raging and their emotions are running high. Because of all this energy swirling around the teenager, the teenager themselves could be attracting the activity, and not be aware of it at all.

We quickly dismissed this theory because of the EVPs we'd gotten, and the fact that some of the activity didn't fit the pattern normally associated with a teenage-induced poltergeist.

Randy and I were at our client's home that day to conduct a preliminary walk-through of the property, before bringing in the rest of the team for a full-scale investigation the following weekend.

The clients indicated they really didn't mind the spirits being around the house, but the entity in the basement was too much for them to tolerate. Initially we felt that the violent activity, such as the scratching and pushing, could be attributed to the ex-husband. The energy I'd felt didn't substantiate that theory, but we couldn't as of yet rule out the possibility. The ex-husband had resided in the home, and there had been domestic violence present.

What really caught my attention was the feeling I got as I walked around the yard of the house. It felt as though something was pulling me toward the backyard of the home, which was comprised of acre upon acre of old, overgrown crop fields and treed areas, but I didn't take the time to explore the area until we'd gathered the entire team the following weekend.

We arrived that weekend with the full team in tow, along with another paranormal investigation team we worked with on various cases.

We had plenty of daylight left, so the head of their team, Carrie, and I decided to walk around the vast landscape behind the house, while the teams were busy setting up the technical equipment—which could take a couple of hours.

We trudged through the tall grass and almost obscure trails for about an hour when we ran into the homeowner and one of her daughters, who were out walking the dog.

My personal opinion is that she was keeping an eye on what we were doing, but I can't say for sure.

"You know, there's the foundation of an old building out here somewhere." She took a long drag of her cigarette and blew smoke rings into the air.

"Really?" Carrie and I looked at each other.

"Yeah, one of the neighbors, who lived here forever, told us that back about twenty or thirty or so years ago, there used to be a satanic church on the property. I've only lived here for six years, so I wasn't anywhere near this place at the time the cult was active," Jennifer explained, not meeting our curious gazes.

"Which neighbor? Can we talk to them?" I asked.

"He passed away a few years ago," Jennifer said. "The property has changed hands a lot since then."

Carrie and I looked at each other knowingly. We'd heard rumors for years about a satanic cult that operated in this area back in the late 1960s through the late 1970s—perhaps even into the early 1980s.

While the existence of such a cult is pretty much common knowledge for anyone who lived in that area during the time the cult was active, it's still very difficult to get anyone to talk about what happened back then, for fear of retribution by any cult members who may still be living in the area.

We'd looked for the church rumored to be the main hub of that activity off and on for years, but we had never found it. We were almost ready to chalk it up to urban legend, but too many people we'd talked to over the years had confirmed the existence of such a cult.

"Do you know where it is?" I asked.

"I honestly don't remember, but I know it's out here. From what I've heard, there was a fire out here before I bought the property and the church burned to the ground. All that remains is the stone foundation," Jennifer told us. "Do you think that could have something to do with what is going on at my house?"

"It could," Carrie admitted, not wanting to say much.

"We're going to wander around a little more. We'll meet you back at the house shortly," I said and headed off into a clump of trees, with Carrie close on my heels.

"This could be way bigger than we thought," Carrie mused as we wandered down a trail.

"Yeah, we've got to find that church. I think that could be what's drawing all the activity to this place. But we're running out of daylight, and we don't want to be out here in the dark without any flashlights or other equipment," I added.

Carrie nodded, and we both reluctantly turned around and headed back to the client's house.

I cornered Randy by the cars, and out of the earshot of our client I told him what we'd discovered. Randy agreed with my theory that the negative energy from the old satanic church was only adding to our current problem, and that we didn't have any choice but to move on and try to get rid of what was already here.

Both of us were pretty sure that in time, what we got rid of tonight would only rear its ugly head once again in the future, unless we found that church. However, with darkness falling, and the more immediate concerns of our client, we knew all hopes of finding the satanic church tonight was out of the question.

The members of both ghost hunting teams assembled inside the house and we all paired off, grabbed various pieces of equipment, and headed off in separate directions to investigate.

I took two team members and made a beeline for the barn. There'd been many reports of a male apparition there, along with a rather strange story.

According to reports, the previous owners hired a woman to paint a stallion on the barn while they were on vacation. Upon returning from their trip, there wasn't a stallion painted on the barn, even though the painter had called them to tell them the job was complete.

They contacted the painter, who understandably was very confused as to what happened to the mural she'd painted. She then, in front of witnesses, repainted the stallion mural. The next morning, the mural had disappeared, and there were no signs that it had been painted over. If this story is true, and there's no reason to believe it isn't, we still can't explain what happened to the mural.

The barn itself was small, but adequate enough to hold a couple of horses and a small tack room. It'd fallen into a state of disrepair, and stood painted in faded, chipping, white paint, about a hundred feet from the house.

We opened the barn door and gingerly walked into the barn, testing every footstep to make sure the floor was secure, before proceeding into the interior of the barn.

Piles of old wood stood against the back wall, and an old workbench covered in dust and spiderwebs sat just inside the door, to the right. We scanned the room with our flashlights and noticed the entrance to the loft, right above the workbench. A flimsy excuse for a ladder leaned against the wall, granting access to the loft if we were brave enough to venture up the rickety ladder.

We positioned ourselves in a triangular pattern: I went to the far side of the barn; a team member went at an angle to me, on the left side of the barn; and the other team member stayed by the door. We began an EVP session, to see if any spirits wanted to communicate with us.

I could feel the presence of a male spirit as we worked, but I couldn't pick up on exactly where he was and, other than a few shuffling sounds in the loft, we couldn't make contact. We also couldn't rule out that the noises we heard in the loft weren't caused by an animal, such as a raccoon, or another one of the many critters known to inhabit the area.

As we walked out of the barn to head back into the house, I saw the spirit of a little girl standing with her hands folded in front of her, rocking back and forth pensively on her heels. She was wearing a cute little pink dress that fell mid-calf, with ruffles around the neck and wrists. She was dressed in a style from an era long forgotten. Her blond hair was braided on each side and lay over her shoulders.

Knowing I was the only one who could see her, I left the group and walked over to her.

"Well, hello. What's your name?" I asked.

"Katherine. Are you here to help us?" she asked.

"Yes, honey. What do you need help with?" I knelt down so I was eye level with the little ghost.

"We want to leave, but the bad man won't let us," she said.

"Who's here with you?" I looked around but didn't see any other spirits.

"My mommy and daddy and my brother, Jacob—he's three," Katherine said.

"I see. What bad man won't let you leave?" I asked.

"He lives down there," Katherine pointed to the outside door to the basement.

"Yes, I know of this man. I'll take care of it so you and your family can leave," I promised. "Why is your whole family here?"

"We got the fever. My brother died, then my daddy, then me and Mommy." Katherine wiped a phantom tear from her eye.

Her information told me that she lived on this property in the late 1880s or the early 1900s, as those were the times plagues of scarlet fever ravaged the population in the area.

"That was a long time ago," I told her. "Why didn't you all leave before the bad man came?"

"We did. But my brother and I came back here a lot so we could play in the fields. Mommy and Daddy came with us to keep an eye on us," Katherine explained.

"I see. So when you came back the last time the bad man was here, and you couldn't leave, right?" I asked.

"Exactly!" Katherine smiled. "You are going to help us, right?"

"Yes, I will. But you have to promise to stay hidden with your family until it's time for you to go, okay?"

"Okay. We'll stay in the barn. The bad man doesn't come out there a lot."

"Good girl. You run along now. See you later." I smiled as the cute little spirit disappeared as she skipped over to the barn.

I rejoined the team in the house and told them about my encounter with Katherine. We all realized the stakes had just been raised—we had to get rid of the dark entity in the basement—not just for our client's sake, but for the well-being of the family of ghosts that were being held here, against their will.

Pushing forward, Randy, the client, and I made our way upstairs to the client's bedroom. She'd reported hearing laughter coming from the attic area that she was using as a closet, as well as seeing the ghost of her deceased brother-in-law, Michael.

She'd heard the ghost in the closet laugh a few times, but the presence of her brother-in-law was really disturbing her. She wasn't sure what he wanted or why he was there.

Armed with this information, Randy began to video tape, while I walked around the room trying to get a sense of the energy. It didn't take long to pick up on the ghost of Michael, because he came forward almost immediately.

He indicated telepathically that he was there to protect our client and her daughters from the entity in the basement. Michael went on to say that the entity in the basement was bad, and that it was responsible for the violent physical attacks on our client and her youngest daughter. While he didn't believe the basement phantom was his brother, he wasn't positive.

I asked him if the dark entity in the basement was a demon, and he responded that he didn't know—he'd never seen it. He'd tried several times to make it leave, but he didn't have any success, as the phantom in the basement was much more powerful than himself.

Michael also told me that he was now trapped here by the entity in the basement. He'd started out trying to make sure our client and her girls were safe in case the ghost of her deceased husband showed up, because he knew how violent his brother had been in life and was fearful of what harm his brother could cause in death. He never expected to run across something like what lived in the basement, but didn't know if it was his brother or not—although he doubted it.

When asked about the ghost in the closet, which would laugh at his sister-in-law, he admitted that it was him and said he meant no harm; he was just trying to let her know he was here. He would hang out in the closet to give her some privacy.

After promising to help him, Randy and I went back downstairs to where we'd set up our command center. I paired off with a couple of our female investigators and decided to investigate the youngest daughter's bedroom, where a lot of the activity seemed to take place.

When we first entered the bedroom, it was deathly quiet and almost devoid of energy. This caught our attention because the bedroom was on the first floor and with all the investigators running around the property, the bedroom should have been noisy. Yet it felt as if we just entered some kind of dark, empty abyss.

We shined our flashlights around the room, and I noticed some pill bottles on the vanity. Closer inspection revealed they were antidepressants. I left my teammates to investigate, and went out to the living room to ask our client about this. She confirmed that her daughter had been very depressed in the last year and was taking the medication; this was a valuable clue.

My research and my own experience has been that a depressed teenager who lives in the home where paranormal activity is occurring, could draw in negative entities.

The teenager is not doing this consciously of course, but the energy of a teenager, coupled with the fact that they are emitting negative energy in the form of depression, drug or alcohol abuse, etc., can feed some type of entities and invite them into the home.

Demons, poltergeists, and all other types of entities need energy to manifest or cause paranormal activity on Earth. Thus they will "feed" off of any energy source available— and what better source of energy than a teenager.

This could be what drew the entity in the basement to our client's home, and explain why it seemed to focus its attention on the youngest daughter. At that moment, I became more determined than ever to make sure that whatever had taken up residence in their basement was gone before we left that night.

I rejoined my teammates in the bedroom. The energy felt different this time; the air felt charged with electricity, and my teammates were staring intently into the thermal camera.

"There's a dark orb showing up on the thermal camera, but it's not visible to the naked eye. It appears to be casually moving around the bed," they told me.

I looked at the screen of the thermal camera and instantly saw the black orb in question. It wasn't moving fast, just kind of hanging around.

"Let's see if it's intelligent." I sat on the edge of the bed and held out my hand. "Watch the screen and tell me where it is about every three seconds."

My teammates positioned the camera to where they could see me and the orb in the small screen.

"We know you're here. We can see you in the device that one of our investigators is holding in her hand," I told the orb. "Can you come into my hand?"

"It's moving toward you. It's at the end of the bed," Katy, our investigator, told me.

"No one's here to hurt you. Just come into my hand and make contact," I said.

"It's coming closer to you. It's right over your hand, by about two feet," Katy reported.

"Just a little bit more," I urged.

"It's lowering itself down to your hand," Katy said. "It's getting closer ... closer ... bingo!"

Just as Katy spoke, I felt something cold rest in my cupped hand.

"Thank you," I told the orb. "Can you tell me who you are and why you're here?"

As soon as I spoke I felt the coldness leave and the room become void of energy once again.

"It just vanished," Katy said, turning slowly around and scanning the room with the thermal camera for any sign of the black orb. "I didn't see it leave your hand and go anywhere, it just disappeared."

"Apparently it didn't want to engage," I shrugged as I rose off the bed. "But at least we know it was an intelligent entity. If I had to guess, I'd say it was whatever is living in the basement."

My teammates nodded in agreement, and we went to rejoin the team at the command center in the kitchen.

Randy approached me as I entered the kitchen area. "Let's go talk outside," he whispered.

I followed him outside. We walked out into the yard and settled ourselves on the picnic table.

"What's going on?" I asked, twisting open a bottle of water and taking a long drink.

"Some of the investigators have reported seeing a dark shadow down in the basement. It seems to hang around the old fieldstone wall, where we saw it during our preliminary investigation. The investigators have also reported feeling that the energy down there is heavy and dark. One team said something growled at them while they were in the small room at the bottom of the basement stairs."

"Yeah, I think it's time to make whatever is down there leave," I said. "Gather the team in the basement while I get what I need out of my car." I went out to my Jeep and retrieved my ghost hunting kit. A few minutes later, I joined the team and the client in the basement.

The basement of our client's house is only accessible from the outside of the house; it was probably used as a root cellar when the house was originally built. It's divided into three spaces: a small room across from the stairs; a long room to the left of the stairs; and then another alcove off that room. The small room and the long room are divided by a very old fieldstone wall.

Our client told us there was a rumor that someone was buried in the fieldstone wall. While I doubted that, at this point nothing would surprise me, given the type of activity the client was experiencing.

"Okay, I want everyone to stand close together in this area," I pointed to a large space just at the entrance to the alcove. "I'm going to put a circle of salt around you. This is to protect you from whatever negative entity is down here. No matter what happens, you cannot leave the circle. Understand?"

They all nodded in agreement and gathered together in the place I'd indicated. I retrieved a box of sea salt from my ghost hunting kit and began to enclose them in the circle. Sea salt is known in the paranormal world as a means of protection. It's believed that no type of negative entity can cross a line of salt.

I use sea salt all the time when ghost hunting, because when I'm trying to get rid of a dark entity I need that entity to come to me and not to anyone else. Dark entities are unpredictable and can be extremely violent, especially when someone is trying to get rid of them. I make them come after me, because I don't want to have to worry about anyone else present falling under attack. If the dark entity comes after me, I know how to handle it.

While I was doing that, Randy was turning on the ghost box to capture any EVPs during the ritual. A ghost box scans radio frequencies and it's believed that a ghost, spirit, or other type of entity can manipulate the frequencies to form words. We've used it in the past, with great success.

When I finished with the circle of salt, I started to walk into the alcove. Just as I walked by the ghost box, it said, "You're going to die." There was an audible gasp from the people in the circle.

"Not tonight," I responded, looking down at the ghost box.

I continued into the alcove and opened up my kit. I pulled out a lighter and a sage smudge stick and lit it—blowing out the flame, so there was only smoke. Then I grabbed my bottle of holy water. I poured some of the holy water onto the floor at the entrance of the alcove, hoping it would prevent the entity from escaping to another part of the house. As I did that, I asked God to protect all of those present from the dark entity that had invaded this space.

To tell the truth, I really wasn't happy with the situation. I wasn't sure if I was dealing with a malevolent human spirit or some type of inhuman entity, such as a demon. Plus, I was about to break my golden rule of ghost hunting: If you don't know what it is, don't mess with it.

However, I felt I didn't have any other choice. There was too much riding on my getting rid of this being, not just for the safety of the family, but to allow the other spirits trapped here to move on and cross over to the other side.

Satisfied that everything was ready, I turned my attention to the dark entity. I could feel its energy building up in the corner of the alcove. The air felt dark and heavy, and in my mind's eye I saw a dark creature or spirit—I wasn't sure which, huddled up in the corner. I knew it was just sitting there waiting, sizing up its competition—or prey—depending on your point of view, I suppose. The tension and apprehension in the air was almost palpable.

With the smudge stick in hand, I began to walk around the area, to begin the purification and cleansing process. As I walked, I asked God to guide this wayward entity to where it belonged, and to clean the space of negative energy and replace it with His divine white light. After this, I turned my full attention to the entity.

"Okay. Here's how it's going to go," I began. "Either you're going to leave on your own or I'm going to force you out. The choice is yours."

Just as I finished saying that, a strong wall of energy came rushing toward me, and before I could get out of the way, it hit me full force and pushed me against the cement wall.

One of the investigators happened to be taking photographs at the time and, upon review, we saw a gray mist slamming against me.

"I see you've made your choice," I said glibly, as I recovered from the blow and walked back to the middle of the room.

I set the smudge stick on an upside-down pail on the floor in the corner of the alcove. It was right by where the entity retreated after attacking, so I figured the smudge stick might help keep it in its place, and not attack again.

I reached into my bag and pulled out a piece of paper with a powerful spiritual warfare prayer printed on it, and grabbed my bottle of holy water.

As I recited the prayer, I sprinkled a liberal amount of holy water in the corner of the alcove and on the fieldstone wall.

Near the end of the prayer, I felt the entity leave, but I continued on to finish the prayer, in order to have closure and to make sure the entity was gone.

As soon as I finished the prayer, the child spirit, Katherine, appeared at my side. "Can my family and I leave now?" She looked up at me with hope written all over her cherubic face.

"Yes, honey. You can go now. It's safe. You're free," I told her.

"Thank you!" she squealed, and threw her arms around my waist. I could feel the coldness of her touch, but I could also feel the relief in her spirit.

"You're welcome, sweetie," I called after her, as I saw her and her family go up through the ceiling and into the light.

I told everyone they could leave the circle, and we all filed quietly up the basement stairs, into the cool of the evening. Randy and I walked over to the picnic table and sat down.

"I have to clean the rest of the house—just to make sure. Then we're done," I told him.

"Let's do it," Randy said, as he rose from the table. The hour was late, and we were exhausted.

I went downstairs to retrieve my equipment and smudge stick, and proceeded to smudge the entire house. Then I went back through and blessed the house with the holy water.

I'm happy to report that our client says most of the paranormal activity in her house has stopped. While she still sees the spirit of her brother-in-law, Michael, all the other spirits have left.

Our team, Black River Paranormal, is planning a return trip to the property to try and find the remains of the satanic church and to make sure all is well so our client and any spirits on the property can exist in peace.

While I still can't say for sure that the entity in the basement was demonic, I can't rule it out, either. Given the entity's reaction to the prayer and holy water, my best guess is that it was a diabolical entity; however, it's possible that a very dark human spirit could display the same reaction to holy objects and prayers.

If indeed the information told to our client is correct, and the remains of the satanic church are on the property, that's a game changer. The odds would be that if the entity in the basement was a demon, then it is likely to return at some point, or another demon could come forth and take its place.

The only people who know what happened at that church are the ones who attended it, and if they were practicing Satanism, then the energy from whatever rituals they performed would linger for an extremely long period of time.

Since demons, like any other type of entity, need to feed in order to survive, the most likely source of that energy would be from the living—more specifically, our client's family and their neighbors.

Only time will tell if the entity in the basement of that house will return, but if or when it does, we'll be ready for it.

CONCLUSION

It is my sincere hope that you've enjoyed your adventures in the paranormal basement, and that you will return again to further partake in the unique world of the supernatural. I sure had a lot of fun putting this together for you.

As I worked on this book, it forced me to think back on all the ghosts I've met and the experiences I've had. It's been my honor and privilege to have encountered so many ghosts and spirits—even the bad ones.

I genuinely believe that ghosts and spirits are some of the most misunderstood and most feared beings who inhabit our space, and in most cases where paranormal activity is occurring, there's no reason to be afraid. But we, as humans, are often afraid of something we don't understand or have knowledge about.

Thanks to movies and television shows, many people have become conditioned to fear the paranormal, and do not embrace it for what it is. The word *paranormal* is generally defined as something that can't be explained by traditional science. That's a pretty broad definition, if you really think about it.

How many things are in this world, which we really don't understand? Plenty, yet very few people fear other unknown things as much as they fear encounters with ghosts or spirits. I hope this book has helped you to understand that in reality, most ghosts and spirits are just like the living; in fact most ghosts were once alive in human form, too. It's just that now they are in a different form—and they are basically the same person they were when they were alive. So, that being the case, there's really nothing to fear. I hope I've given you a clearer understanding about how ghosts and spirits behave, and a small glimpse into their reality.

Some of the dearly departed who've returned in spirit form I even count among my friends. Kind of creepy, I know, but creepy is pretty much my version of normal. Hardly a day goes by when I don't see or communicate with the spirit world, and I wouldn't have it any other way.

Some of these encounters teach me something, others are pure enjoyment, and still others are a little scary. However, my life is never boring. If, for some reason, my gift of being able to see and communicate with spirits suddenly disappeared, I would have a void in my life and in my soul, which nothing else would be able to fill.

I also hope that you have taken something away from each and every story in this book—whether it's a lesson, or just pure enjoyment. Keep in mind that these stories span my lifetime of being thrust into the world of the paranormal—whether I wanted to go along for the ride or not. Such is the life of a psychic medium, and other people who have special gifts. If you've been blessed with such a gift, I hope you embrace it and not try to outrun, ignore, or turn away from it.

There is so much work to be done in the world of the paranormal, and there are so many people who need to be helped dealing with their own ghostly activity. That is my calling—to help as many people as I can.

My goal is to educate people about the paranormal and assist people who feel they are being haunted. It is my passion and my life's work.

If you have any questions or comments, or need help with your own special ghost or paranormal activity, please don't hesitate to contact me at debichestnut@yahoo.com. You can also visit my website at www.myparanormaladvisor.com.

Until next time, my friends, Happy Hauntings!

To Write to the Author

If you wish to contact the author or would like more information about this book, please write to the author in care of Llewellyn Worldwide Ltd. and we will forward your request. Both the author and publisher appreciate hearing from you and learning of your enjoyment of this book and how it has helped you. Llewellyn Worldwide Ltd. cannot guarantee that every letter written to the author can be answered, but all will be forwarded. Please write to:

Debi Chestnut
℅ Llewellyn Worldwide
2143 Wooddale Drive.
Woodbury, MN 55125-2989, U.S.A.

Please enclose a self-addressed stamped envelope for reply, or $1.00 to cover costs. If outside the USA, enclose an international postal reply coupon.

GET MORE AT LLEWELLYN.COM

Visit us online to browse hundreds of our books and decks, plus sign up to receive our e-newsletters and exclusive online offers.

- Free tarot readings • Spell-a-Day • Moon phases
- Recipes, spells, and tips • Blogs • Encyclopedia
- Author interviews, articles, and upcoming events

GET SOCIAL WITH LLEWELLYN

Find us on Facebook

www.Facebook.com/LlewellynBooks

Follow us on **twitter**™

www.Twitter.com/Llewellynbooks

GET BOOKS AT LLEWELLYN

LLEWELLYN ORDERING INFORMATION

Order online: Visit our website at www.llewellyn.com to select your books and place an order on our secure server.

Order by phone:
- Call toll free within the U.S. at 1-877-NEW-WRLD (1-877-639-9753)
- Call toll free within Canada at 1-866-NEW-WRLD (1-866-639-9753)
- We accept VISA, MasterCard, and American Express

Order by mail:
Send the full price of your order (MN residents add 6.875% sales tax) in U.S. funds, plus postage and handling to: Llewellyn Worldwide, 2143 Wooddale Drive Woodbury, MN 55125-2989

POSTAGE AND HANDLING

STANDARD (U.S. & Canada):
(Please allow 12 business days)
$25.00 and under, add $4.00.
$25.01 and over, FREE SHIPPING.

INTERNATIONAL ORDERS (airmail only):
$16.00 for one book, plus $3.00 for each additional book.

Visit us online for more shipping options. Prices subject to change.

FREE CATALOG!

To order, call
1-877-NEW-WRLD
ext. 8236
or visit our website